Shalom, Golda

Shalom,

Golda

by Terry Morris

HAWTHORN BOOKS, INC.
Publishers
New York

TYPE DESIGN BY MARTIN J. BAUMANN

1   2   3   4   5   6   7   8   9   10

To Israel, with love

Preface

In the late afternoon of Tuesday, May 19, 1970, I sat in the visitor's chair beside the desk of the Prime Minister of Israel, Golda Meir, in Jerusalem. Her secretary had introduced me, remained for a few minutes' chat, and then left us alone for an uninterrupted one-and-a-half-hour interview.

During twenty years of free-lance writing I had interviewed people of every sort in many parts of the world, but I had never felt before, as I did then, that I was in the presence of a great and unique human being. Much has been made of the Prime Minister as a Jewish mother and grandmother, and undoubtedly her maternal feelings are deep and abiding. Much, too, has been made of her lifelong dedication to Labor Zionism and her extraordinary record of achievement before and after the state of Israel was born. But as we ranged over the material of this book, what most impressed and moved me about Golda Meir was the moral and spiritual fiber of this strong yet gentle woman —her profound belief in the dignity of man and her compassionate concern for the quality of life.

The people of Israel are, of course, her first care, but her heart and mind go out to people everywhere and particularly to young people in whom, as she said to me, the courage to dream of a better world and the will to help make it so must be kept alive and nourished. Coming from Golda Meir, this is not a preachment but a statement that describes her own more than threescore years of daring to dream and investing all her formidable strength and conviction into realizing her vision of a Jewish National Home.

To Golda Meir, helping create and safeguard the state of Israel was always and continues to be a labor of love. So was the writing of this book to me. And so, let us hope, will the reading of it be to those young people with whom the Prime Minister has bridged the generation gap by her love.

T. M.
New York City

Acknowledgments

Among the delights of writing this book, the principal one was the privilege of meeting Golda Meir, but I was also greatly privileged to meet and talk with her sister, Clara Stern, and with many of Mrs. Meir's longtime friends and associates in Israel, who provided me with invaluable live source material about her personal life and public career: Simcha Dinitz and Lou Kadar, political and personal secretaries to the Prime Minister; Regina Hamburger Medzini; Eiga Shapiro; Judge Zvi Bar-Niv; Zalman Chen; Ezra Danin; Ben Rabinovitsch; and Shalamit Unna. Many thanks, also, to the archivists at the Jerusalem *Post* and to the Zionist Archives and *Hadassah Magazine* in New York for their assistance. For photographs I am indebted to the Government Press Office in Tel Aviv, the Israel Office of Information in New York City, and the Zionist Archives in New York City.

T. M.

Contents

Preface   v

Acknowledgments   vii

List of Illustrations   xi

1. In My Father's House   1

2. Running toward Something   8

3. "At Last I Have My Freedom!"   20

4. It's Difficult to Be a Jew   29

5. Palestine: The Naked Land   38

6. Some of the Happiest Years   48

7. "For Such a Woman There Is No Rest"   58

8. Histadrut   66

9. "Therein Lies Our Strength"   74

10. Survivors of the Holocaust   84

11. The Will to Resist   94

12. "They Shall No More Be Plucked Out of Their Land"   103

13. "The Most Passionate Zionist Speech
    I Have Ever Heard!"   113

14. "Let's Have *More* Jews!"   123

15. "Golda Is the Best Man in My Cabinet"   136

16. Who Better Than a Jew Understands
    African Problems?   146

17. The Golda Era   155

18. "Israel Is So Big in Spite of Its Smallness!"   166

19. What Can You Do? She's Irresistible!   177

Epilogue: Open End   190

Bibliography   195

Index   197

List of Illustrations

Golda as a young child in Pinsk   3

Golda, sixteen, in Denver   18

Golda   27

At a Shavuot picnic with young Milwaukee Zionists   34

Kiryath Anavim   46

Feeding the chickens at Merhavia   53

Golda in her early thirties   62

As troubleshooter for Histadrut   71

Three orphans   76

Youth from Germany arrive in Tel Aviv   85

Golda speaking to young settlers   95

Grandmother Golda   104

Soviet Jews greet Israel's ambassador   120

Young refugees at a Yemenite tent camp   125

*With President Itzhak Ben-Zvi and Prime Minister Moshe
Sharett* 137

*Foreign Minister Golda Meir at an Afro-Asian seminar in
Haifa* 151

The Prime Minister wheels her newest grandchild 156

Golda at the grave of a boy killed in Kiryat Shemona 170

*The Prime Minister and the President
of the United States* 184

In a Milwaukee schoolroom 191

Shalom, Golda

CHAPTER 1

In My Father's House

EVEN AS A very young child, Golda Mabovitz became aware of the terror and repression that periodically bore down upon the Jews huddled within the ghettos of czarist Russia. The terror and repression bred into her a horror of helplessness and dependency which began in 1902, when Golda was four. She still remembers standing on the steps of a house in Kiev, in the Russian Ukraine, with other children her age. She watched her father and the fathers of the neighbors' children boarding up doors and windows as protection against a threatened Cossack pogrom. All the children were silent. The only sound was the knocking of hammers. She did not know exactly what was happening, but she felt that it was something serious and dangerous. Then the fathers gave their children sticks with which to defend themselves, and she was very frightened because she knew how useless it would be even to try.

The Cossacks did not come on that particular day, but in April of the following year, 1903, the notorious Kishinev pogrom took place. Forty-five men, women, and children were killed, and more than one thousand homes and shops were looted and destroyed. In protest, the whole Jewish community decided to fast for a day in the synagogue. Despite her parents' objections that she was much too young, Golda fasted, too. Her parents began to suspect, and correctly, that she had inherited the iron will of her great-grandmother, to whom everyone had come for counsel and advice until her death at the age of ninety-four.

Then, on Bloody Sunday of 1905, more hideous pogroms swept the ghettos of Russia when Jews were made the scapegoats for the farmers and workers who had marched to the Czar's palace and peacefully petitioned for a constitution, only to be shot down and massacred.

It was open season for hunting Jews. Golda, then seven, was playing with a friend on a street in Pinsk when a drunken peasant grabbed them and banged their heads together.

"That's what we'll do with the Jews," he said, laughing raucously. "We'll knock their heads together and we'll be finished with them!"

She was terrified and her head ached, but she did not cry. Tears offered no relief for the anger and frustration she felt. Was that what being a Jew meant? To hammer boards against windows and arm little children with sticks? Why must Jews cower and cringe? Why could not Jews stand erect with dignity and pride in their Jewishness? She had none of the answers. All she knew was that she must never forget the sound of the hammers, the hoofs of Cossack horses on the cobblestoned streets, or the drunken laughter of the peasant.

In a few respects her family fared better than other ghetto Jews because her father, Moshe Mabovitz, was a skilled carpenter who had been given permission to live among the gentiles outside the pale, or ghetto, in the city of Kiev. He made fine furniture, but he had no head for business, and being a Jewish craftsman, he had no recourse to the courts when his workers or customers cheated him. These were among the bitter facts of life for a Jew in czarist Russia. Early and lastingly Golda absorbed them and never forgot the insecurity, poverty, and rootlessness such a way of life bred.

Golda (center) as a young child in Pinsk; Shana, her elder sister; and their mother, holding the baby of the family, Clara

Within a year of their marriage Golda's father and mother, Moshe and Blume Mabovitz, had a daughter, Shana. Five more babies were born, but they fell victims to the dreadfully high infant-mortality rate in the ghettos. Golda's birth and survival after so many tragic deaths made her the family pet until, four years later, another daughter, Clara, became the baby of the family.

Mr. Mabovitz continually tried to make what he called fresh beginnings, and with each of these the family moved, uprooting themselves from one dark hole only to set themselves down again in a worse one. By 1903 he had had enough of trying to buck pogroms and the discrimination against Jewish craftsmen. Along with thousands of other Russian Jews, he left his family behind and immigrated to the United States. He planned to send for them when he had succeeded in making a living and establishing a home.

Mrs. Mabovitz and her three daughters moved from Kiev to her parents' house in Pinsk, where the Jewish ghetto was a hotbed of radical activity. Shana, who was then fourteen years old, fell in with a group of young people who began to meet at the home of the sister of Chaim Weizmann, a native of Pinsk and already an acknowledged leader of the Zionists. The house and garden were very pleasant and the atmosphere relaxed and friendly. People came to exchange ideas, and gradually Shana began to learn about their political activities, which, for Jews, meant going underground. Soon Shana, a high-spirited, redheaded wisp of a girl, was delivering papers and leaflets and attending secret meetings and rallies.

One of the greatest difficulties in this underground activity was to arrange meeting places without being discovered by the Russian police. A favorite device was for a couple to ask permission to get married, and then, under cover of gathering for the wedding celebration, the young people would listen to revolutionary speeches. When the guard, posted at the door, warned of an intruder or the police, the orchestra started to play and everyone danced. Meetings were also held after Shabbat services at the synagogue whenever the worshipers could cajole the shammash, or sexton, into letting them stay on.

Many meetings were also held in the Mabovitz house. As in most Russian homes the heart of the household was the large kitchen with a tall stove, which almost reached the ceiling, and was used for giving heat as well as for cooking. Above the stove was a broad ledge, and it was here that seven-year-old Golda hid and overheard what Shana and her friends were saying.

At one of the meetings Shana discovered her and brought her down from her hiding place, but instead of cowering, Golda brazened it out.

"If you won't let me listen," she told Shana, "I'll tell everything to Maxim, the policeman."

"What will you tell him?" Shana asked.

"I'll tell him that you and your friends don't want the Czar and his government."

"If you tell him that," Shana warned, "I'll be sent to Siberia."

Golda considered this for a while. She was angry with Shana but not that angry! No, she would not tell, she promised. But she would not promise not to listen again.

Mrs. Mabovitz knew less about these revolutionary activities than did Golda. Her mother had begun to bake cakes at home and then go about the city selling them to rich people. Preoccupied, she had more or less lost track of her eldest daughter's new friends and new interests until one day she returned earlier than usual from her bakery rounds and surprised Shana and her conspirators. She at once ran out into the street and guarded the front door, ready to give warning if a policeman came by. She had reason to panic. The house they lived in was next door to a police station, and many nights the whole household lay awake listening to the screams of boys and girls who were being detained by the police, questioned and beaten mercilessly for their illegal activities. Once she had made her discovery about Shana's involvement, Mrs. Mabovitz, with Golda by her side for company, would sit up in an agony of anxiety until Shana returned from a late meeting. The nights when Shana did not come home until very late and when Golda and her mother sat listening to the screams from the police station were among Golda's most painful recollections.

Remonstrating with Shana was hopeless; she had also inherited the streak of stubbornness that was a family trait. Besides, she had met and fallen in love with a young Socialist leader, Sam Korngold, whom the police were looking for. He had to keep on the move and use disguises. At one secret meeting addressed by Korngold the police broke in and many people were injured and arrested. Shana jumped off the roof and reached home safely. Korngold disappeared, and she was not to have direct word of him for several years.

The mounting tension was too much for Mrs. Mabovitz. She was certain that Shana was bound to get arrested and tortured by the police—a catastrophe for them all. Though Mrs. Mabovitz was not opposed to Shana's ideas, her fears for Shana's safety decided her to leave Russia with her three daughters and to join their father in America, whether or not he was ready for them.

Mr. Mabovitz had been part of the huge immigration wave from eastern Europe which aroused in native-born Americans and established immigrants strong feelings of prejudice against these new "foreigners." The Hebrew Immigrant Aid Society (H.I.A.S.) thought it best to disperse Jews to the interior of the country in order to prevent them from clustering in New York City and its already overcrowded ghettos. H.I.A.S. advised Mr. Mabovitz to go to

Milwaukee and "get a good job." Although he had never heard of Milwaukee, he took the advice and found employment as a railroad carpenter. He was just scraping along but managed to send money to his family in Pinsk and to beg them to be patient. When his wife wrote him about Shana's political activities, he agreed with her that it would be wiser and safer for the whole family to emigrate at once.

And it was not too soon. Before leaving Russia, Mrs. Mabovitz rented a room for herself and the girls with the local shohet—a butcher who killed animals and poultry according to Hebraic law. Now sixteen, Shana was becoming reckless. She prevailed on their landlord's young daughter to join her at meetings held at night in the forest outside the town. It seemed that nothing would stop Shana short of dragging her bodily from the country. This, Mrs. Mabovitz accomplished, with great difficulty, arriving in America in the spring of 1906.

It had been a long, tedious journey by rail to Antwerp and by steamship to Canada. Their baggage had been stolen even before they reached Antwerp, and each of them had only one change of clothing. When at last they reached Milwaukee and were met at the railroad station by Mr. Mabovitz, they were a bedraggled lot, bewildered, exhausted, and disoriented.

The eight-year-old Golda was the first to recover her high spirits. This was America! And she had her father back again! Even before the school term started a few months later, she had picked up enough English to understand others and to make herself understood. To attend school and to learn was high adventure, and the deprivations, fears, and insecurities of her life in Kiev and Pinsk began to fade, even though they were never forgotten.

CHAPTER 2

Running toward Something

IN THE EARLY 1900's Milwaukee was an industrial city producing machinery, textiles, and beer, with a population of about half a million people, of whom some forty thousand were Jews, mostly blue-collar workers except for a sprinkling of well-to-do German-Jewish families, who had become "assimilated" and were disdainful of the recently arrived immigrants from eastern Europe.

Mr. Mabovitz had found an apartment for his family above a hole-in-the-wall store, where his wife opened a grocery, selling milk, rolls, eggs, sugar, and a few other staples. The store was Mrs. Mabovitz's inspiration, but her husband, a proud man, felt it reflected on his ability to make a living for his family, so he would not have any part of shopkeeping and pretended the store did not exist. For their part, the daughters engaged in endless wrangling over whose turn it was to tend the store when their mother could not.

Shana argued loftily from principle. The store was a "capitalist" enterprise, and as a dedicated socialist she could not lend her support. Anyway, she argued, she had not left Russia of her own free will. She insisted on keeping to the old ways, refusing to accept the customs of American girls in dress, language, attitudes, or anything else. She declared that she could find no purpose to life in America; all it offered was materialism and the negation of her own revolutionary philosophy. Whenever her mother succeeded in coercing her into working in the grocery, she hated it and grumbled, "What good was it to come to America for this!"

Clara was, of course, too young to be involved. So it was left to Golda to help most in the store, opening it before going to school, while her mother went to the market to pick up fresh supplies. Often, her mother relieved her too late to get to school on time. The principal summoned Mrs. Mabovitz to school and told her that Golda's tardiness was a serious matter. The mother refused to cooperate. Why, she wanted to know, was arriving at school a little late so important when Golda was a very good student who got high marks?

Golda felt otherwise. At the age of nine or ten she had decided to become a schoolteacher, and her performance in elementary school would count heavily in gaining admittance to high school. She pleaded with her mother, but it was a losing battle. She had to continue to be tardy and received only a B in punctuality, spoiling an otherwise perfect record. Golda deeply resented the demands the store made upon her, and later, when she stole a few coins from the till to buy stamps for Shana, who was then in Denver, she could not really feel bad about it. She had earned the money —the hard way!

Despite the bickering over the grocery, the Mabovitz household was generally bright and pleasant. Her parents were very affectionate toward one another and liked to describe how they had fallen in love at first sight and married over the objections of their parents. On Shabbat, the Jewish Sabbath, they held open house with guests coming and going. Soon their small apartment became a center for other immigrants and even for some of Shana's revolutionary friends who moved to Milwaukee. There was always somebody outside the family at table to discuss community problems, politics, and how things were going in the old country.

Mr. Mabovitz had a fine voice and a repertory of Russian and Yiddish folk songs which he taught his children and, later, his grandchildren.

In 1906, the year the Mabovitzes were reunited, Golda's father joined a union of railroad workers, and on Labor Day he asked his family to stand on a certain street corner and watch him march in the workers' parade. As they stood waiting for the parade to reach their corner, little Clara saw policemen on horseback at the head of the procession. She began to cry and screamed, "Mother, the Cossacks are coming!" She was so upset that they had to take her home, where she was put to bed with a high fever. Golda tried to explain to her little sister that here in America there was freedom, that their father was an organized worker who could march in parades, and that the policemen were there to defend the marchers, not, like the Cossacks in Russia, to disperse them.

America also offered the opportunity to speak out against injustice, as Golda discovered after just two years in the country, when she was only ten years old.

Schoolbooks were not then supplied free, and some of Golda's classmates could not afford to buy them. That was unfair, Golda protested. Why should children be handicapped and discriminated against solely because they were poor? She had been making her own pocket money by teaching English to immigrants at ten cents a lesson, and she used her earnings to help organize other ten-year-olds into the American Young Sister Society to collect money to buy textbooks for the needy. When people refused because they were too poor themselves, Golda reminded them: "I was not exactly born among counts and royalty either!"

Her principal aide was her best friend, Regina Hamburger, whose family had emigrated from Austro-Hungary when she was three and now lived on the same street as the Mabovitzes. The girls had announcements printed of a forthcoming "ball" at Milwaukee's Packen Hall, which they rented for the occasion. The ball, which featured speeches followed by tea and sandwiches, was so successful that it made the front page of the local newspaper.

Golda reviewed the aims of the American Young Sister Society and then recited two poems in Yiddish, her home language. Tall for her age and standing very erect, her heavy chestnut braids swinging, she spoke so feelingly and earnestly that she touched the hearts and pocketbooks of her audience and the public conscience of the newspaper. After complimenting Golda on her speech the paper thanked her and the American Young Sister Society for jogging adults into an awareness of the injustice being done to the city's poor schoolchildren. Accompanying the article was a picture of the society members with the notation: "President Golda Mabovitz, top row, fourth from the right."

To Mr. Mabovitz, who had rigid ideas about what was suitable behavior for his daughters, this debut of Golda's as a champion of worthy causes was something to be proud of. But two years later, when twelve-year-old Golda decided to stand on a wagon and speak at a Milwaukee street corner in behalf of the Socialist party and its leader, Eugene V. Debs, whom she much admired, he was furious. Packen Hall was one thing, but the daughter of a Mabovitz was not going to make speeches in the street.

"You're not going," her father said.

She was as stubborn as he was. "Yes, I am."

"If you do, I'll come and pull you down off the wagon by your braids," he threatened, and Golda knew that he usually kept his word.

Nonetheless, Golda went, but she warned her friends to expect a scandal. After the audience was warmed up by the others, Golda rose to speak, searching the audience for her father but not spotting him. Apparently, he had not come, after all.

When she got home, her mother was waiting for her.

"Where's Father?" Golda asked.

"Oh, he went to bed," her mother said.

"Did he come to hear me speak?"

"Yes, he did."

"Well?"

Her mother smiled. "He said he didn't know where you got it from but that you're a terrific speaker. So he let you alone and came home."

The fire and eloquence that so impressed her father appeared only when she was deeply convinced that what she was saying was the truth and that it needed very much to be said. Also, she always made an effort to make immediate personal contact with her audience, reaching people with her warmth, spontaneity, and concern.

By the time they were twelve years old, Golda and Regina were inseparable. Both girls were tall and looked older than their age, and when they applied to a department store for Saturday jobs as messenger girls, they were not asked embarrassing questions about working papers. When they reached the age of fourteen, they worked all summer in the store, wrapping packages and running errands, nine hours a day for a wage of three dollars a week.

Golda was not only mature-looking for her age, she was mature beyond her years, ripened by the tensions and strife that were then splitting the Mabovitz household into two camps. Shana, who had remained fairly quiescent during the first few years after their arrival in America, decided that she wished to resume her schooling. Her parents were startled at this demand, shocked that a grown girl, and particularly a poor Jewish girl whose parents were having a hard enough time making ends meet, should even think about such a thing! Either she should marry or she should find a job and contribute to the household. But this time Shana did not argue with them. She was of age, and whether they liked it or not, she planned to leave home and fend for herself.

Shana had another strong motive for leaving. She had learned that Sam Korngold, whom she had never forgotten, had succeeded in dodging the Russian police and had made his way to the United States and was living in New York. She learned, also, that he was out of work and very depressed. All he knew how to do was to organize revolutionary underground activity, and there were no help-wanted signs at employment agencies for this form of assistance —not even in America!

Shana wrote to him to come to Milwaukee. She rented a room for him, and as she predicted, he soon found jobs, first in a brewery and then in a cigarette factory. Shana worked in a factory, too, pushing herself far beyond her capacity. At night she and Sam attended school and actively participated in Socialist party meetings. They were extremely happy until Shana collapsed one day and subsequently learned that she had tuberculosis. The doctor prescribed wholesome food, plenty of fresh air, and no work. Reluctantly, Shana had to return to her parents' house.

But Shana's having left home in the first place had caused a rift between her and her parents which was widened by their refusal to accept her friendship with Sam Korngold. To them, he was unsafe—a wild-eyed radical—and, besides, he was even poorer than they were with little prospect of bettering himself, since he had no trade.

For Golda, caught between the two camps within one house and suffering for the pain both sides were feeling, the situation was extremely trying. She loved her parents and she loved her sister, who lay wretchedly in bed for at least part of the day, coughing and spitting blood. She had met Sam and recognized him for a warmhearted, compassionate human being who was utterly devoted to Shana. She would have liked to have him as her big brother.

Shana's condition worsened, and she left for Denver where the Jewish Hospital for Consumptives offered the care she desperately needed. Within a year Sam Korngold joined Shana in Denver, and they were married. While washing dishes at the hospital during the day, he learned the dry-cleaning and laundry business at night and hoped soon to open a store of his own.

Shana and her parents did not correspond, but Golda wrote to her sister regularly and in order not to offend her parents, carried on the correspondence secretly, using the addresses of friends as a mail drop to receive Shana's replies. Golda continued to enjoy a loving and close relationship with her parents until her graduation from elementary school approached.

Mrs. Mabovitz had never taken seriously Golda's announcement that she wished to go not only to high school but also to normal school to train as a teacher. To the mother Golda's plans were a child's idle talk, amounting only to unrealistic idealism and stargazing. But Mrs. Mabovitz was wrong on two counts. Golda never talked idly and was a practical idealist, always ready to translate her idealism into action. Still, her mother was right in that Golda was a stargazer to whom realism meant the courage to dream and then the will to do whatever was necessary to make the dream come true.

"Only those who dare, who have the courage to dream, can really accomplish something," she confided to Regina. "People who are forever asking themselves: 'Is it realistic? Can it be accomplished? Is it worth trying?' accomplish nothing that's really worthwhile or imaginative. What's realistic? A stone? Something that's already in existence? That's not realism. That's death. It's stagnation."

To her mother, such passionate striving would have been incomprehensible. When Golda graduated, Mrs. Mabovitz attended the ceremonies and indulgently listened to her daughter make the class valedictorian speech. She heard Golda declare that preparation for living a life that was intellectually and socially useful was the highest purpose of education and that to fulfill one's greatest potential in both these respects was the best way of giving thanks for the wonderful opportunity a free education in America offered.

Fine! Mrs. Mabovitz thought. Fine words. Surely Golda was a gifted speaker! But there were more important things than this, her mother thought. Her daughter was a fourteen-year-old with the carriage and bearing of a young woman. She was a lovely girl with clear, fair skin, naturally curly chestnut hair, and deep-set, clear gray eyes. Such a girl rated a good marriage with a man of substance who could care for her properly so that she could live like a lady. But a schoolteacher? Who needed it? Not only did a man not want a girl who was better educated and smarter than he was, but a schoolteacher might just as well resign herself to being single for the rest of her life.

Also, she had a man in mind for Golda. A man with good prospects, not like the pack of poor young devils who were always buzzing around Golda. True, the man was a good bit older than her daughter, but he was already prospering as a lawyer. He was not a carpenter like Golda's father, God bless him, or even a merchant like the man her own parents had wanted her to marry, but a professional man! Golda had only to snap her fingers and he would come running. In a year or two, why not marriage?

To Golda, all of this was the sheerest nonsense. She was going to high school and then to teacher-training school, and that was that!

Regina Hamburger also looked forward to high school, and although her parents did not object as strenuously as Golda's, they were not happy about the idea. She and her parents hit on a compromise: She would attend business school for two years, learning typing and shorthand, and high school, if she insisted, at night. But Golda was not prepared to make a similar compromise. She had worked hard, made an excellent record, and earned the privilege of going to high school. Besides, she had helped out in the store and earned her own pocket money since she was ten. She saw no reason why she should not go as far as her abilities could take her.

She enrolled in high school for the fall term of 1912 and went doggedly ahead despite her mother's daily expressions of disapproval. As her mother's nagging increased, so did the flow of clandestine correspondence between Golda and the Korngolds in Denver, from whom she received full sympathy and support. When Golda wrote that her mother's needling was getting under her skin and interfering with her performance at school, they stepped up their encouragement and hinted that in Denver she would not have to suffer from such handicaps. By this time Shana was cured of tuberculosis, she had a baby daughter, and Sam had opened his own store. In early November of 1912 Sam Korngold wrote Golda telling her that he and Shana would be glad to have her live with them. He promised her "all the opportunities to study, plenty to eat, and . . . the necessary clothes a person ought to have."

Golda was torn but not for long. Of course, she would have to leave home secretly, for her parents would never let her go. Someday, she felt, they would understand that she was running toward something, not away from them. Now, she knew, they would suffer and think that she did not love them, else how could she hurt them like this? Yet, no matter how hard she searched her conscience, Golda could not feel that what she was about to do was wrong. She would go to Denver!

Regina was in her confidence and shared in the plotting and planning. How to find the ways and means? Both of them had saved money from their summer work in the department store, and Regina contributed as much of her savings as she could possibly spare. A friendly neighbor loaned Golda a few dollars, and the Korngolds managed to send the rest of her train fare. At last she was free to go.

Her bedroom was one flight up from street level, and she planned to tie a rope around her packed suitcase and lower it to Regina. Just as she opened her window, Regina's brother came by and saw his sister idly standing in the street for no apparent reason. It was a dark night, for which the girls were grateful, but Regina's brother did not think his sister should be out by herself.

"What're you doing here?" he asked.

Regina swallowed. "Oh, I'm waiting for Golda. She'll be right down."

Her brother hesitated, then shrugged and moved on. As soon as he was out of sight, Golda lowered the suitcase, and Regina whisked it off into some deep bushes nearby.

Next morning, Golda tucked some school books under her arm and pretended to be going off to school as usual. Instead, she picked up the suitcase and headed for the railroad station. To avoid suspicion, Regina did not cut her classes to see Golda off. At the station Golda mailed a postcard telling her parents what she had done and promising to write as soon as she was settled in at Shana and Sam's.

But that afternoon, when she did not return from school at the usual time, Mrs. Mabovitz went to Regina's home to ask if she knew where Golda was.

"Oh," Regina said as casually as she could, "Golda's gone to Denver."

Mrs. Hamburger gave her daughter a few hard smacks for her part in the plot, but Regina, expecting to be punished, thought it was unimportant so long as Golda was safely on her way.

Actually, Golda was still in the railroad station waiting for a train. Sitting miserably alone on a bench, she was

Golda, sixteen, with Shana and Sam Korngold and their child in Denver

furious with herself for being such a fool. Why hadn't she thought of checking a timetable? Why had she assumed that once she was ready to travel, the right train would come along? What if her parents came after her? But she did not need to worry on that score. The Mabovitzes were just as naïve about railroad schedules as she was.

It was a long wait, but what lay ahead proved to be worth waiting for.

CHAPTER 3

"At Last I Have My Freedom!"

When Golda arrived in Denver, she was so bursting with life and poured such tireless energy into experiencing and enjoying it that the Korngolds laughed and said the high altitude had gone to her head.

She entered the local high school and had no difficulty reaching and maintaining her usual high standard. After school she cheerfully ironed shirts and dresses in Sam's store as the very least she could do to repay the Korngolds for their hospitality. Shana was delighted to have been able to rescue her young sister from what she described, typically, as "the tyranny and oppression" of their parents. The Korngolds opened their home to the considerable colony of impoverished intellectuals who were or had been patients at the hospital. Most were immigrants from eastern Europe, and many of the young men, to Golda's delight, were unmarried and several years older than she, just older enough to look up to. All of them shared a passion for talk, endless glasses of tea, and the conviction that the world was in desperate need of change. But there the unanimity ended. How to change the world, to what degree, and by which means were the subject of arguments far into the night.

Although she was not shy, Golda at first took little active part in these discussions. She knew she was out of her depth, and her response, when this happened, was to listen with such concentration that she could repeat almost verbatim what she had heard. But she was not interested in parroting other people's arguments. What were they really saying? Did it make sense to her? Could she go along with it?

In Russia the underground Marxist revolutionaries had done their work well, and most of the visitors in the Korngolds' parlor had been exposed to their theories. Some of them firmly believed in dialectical materialism, the theory that changes come about as the result of conflicts between the classes, especially between the capitalists, who own the means of production, and the workers, whose labor they exploit. Inevitably, these clashes result in the overthrow of the capitalists and a take-over of the means of production by the workers who would own them in common, thereby creating a classless society. Was not dialectical materialism, therefore, the only logical method of historical analysis, one that offered the most hopeful prospect of a better world?

Not at all, said others. Dialectical materialism was derived in the first place from the philosophy of George Wilhelm Friedrich Hegel, who had not lived to see how Marxists were perverting his ideas into an exclusively economic view of society. Were not ideals at least as important as a grub's-eye view of life? In Hegel, his supporters shouted, pausing only for another sip of scalding tea, one had an all-embracing, unified view of the world as being in a constant state of flux, of perpetual self-creation. A philosophy like Hegel's, which welded together theories of ethics, aesthetics, history, politics, and religion, was soul-satisfying, for man cannot live by bread alone.

It was heady stuff which Golda, listening as intently as she could, found mind-expanding, even though she could not follow all of it. But if these young men and women had been able to teach themselves, so could she; after all, the public library was available to her, too.

Several of the visitors at the Korngolds' were adherents of the philosophy of Arthur Schopenhauer, the German philosopher who was considered the father of pessimism. Schopenhauer insisted that what men called will was only a blind, impelling force over which they had virtually no control. All anyone could do about it was to negate the will and embrace science and art as a temporary escape from pain.

For once, Golda stopped listening. Such nonsense! How could a person live except through the exercise of his will, providing, of course, that he did not seek to put down anyone else and that he took the rights of others into consideration? Men were impelled by a force from within, but this force in Golda's view was not blind, like an animal's instinct. What was the human intellect for except to guide the will to do its bidding? How could one live a life that offered only the absence of things, a void? Nothing could be more self-destructive!

Other discussions concerned the current movement for the emancipation of women. The most important demand, just then, was for women's right to vote, and here there were no disagreements except over the antics of the suffragettes, who, among other attention-getting devices, were chaining themselves to lampposts. Certainly the right to vote—to elect and to participate in the government that ruled women's lives as well as men's—was basic.

But there was far less agreement over the women's protest against the prevailing double standard of morality, which condoned premarital sex experience in the case of men but branded a woman who engaged in the sex act before marriage as a scarlet woman, a hussy, a prostitute, and so on. Either chastity should be demanded of both sexes, or it should not be demanded of either!

Shana tended to look nervously at her fifteen-year-old sister whenever sex was discussed, but Golda was only interested in playing the field among the young bachelors who came to open house at the Korngolds'. She enjoyed going with them to meetings, and an occasional picnic or concert. What Golda liked best about these dates was going to a nearby coffee shop with a group after a lecture and sitting up half the night talking over what they had heard.

Shana began to fuss. "You're still a schoolgirl, Golda, and your first duty is to your schoolwork. How can you expect to be alert on a few hours' sleep? You'll wreck your health, for another thing."

Golda heard her out impatiently and then pointed out that her marks were still first-rate and she had never felt in better health.

Shana paid no attention. "Also," she added, "you don't suppose, do you, that these young men you date are interested only in your mind? You're too free with them, Golda. You act as though they're your chums, the way you would act with a girl friend. They'll think you're an easy mark and behave accordingly. They won't respect you."

"And why shouldn't men and women be able to be chums?" Golda demanded. "Why shouldn't it be possible for them to have close friendships on an equal footing? Anyway, I'm not the type to be coy and simpering."

Shana refused to be brushed off. "You don't understand," she stormed. "You're always so sure of yourself, so high and mighty, you won't take advice from anybody—not even from me. I'm only thinking of your own good."

Poor Shana, Golda thought. Despite everything she says she believes, in another few years she'll be as conventional as any of the bourgeois housewives she's so scornful of! What an irony! Shana, the revolutionary, was becoming straitlaced and puritanical.

Shana was becoming increasingly critical of Golda, almost obsessive in her feeling that her sister was headed for disaster. From time to time, Sam intervened and tried to temper Shana's scoldings, pointing out that Golda was a sensible girl, not at all flighty, and worthy of their trust. All he accomplished was to turn Shana's anger onto himself.

Golda's position in the family constellation was a sensitive and difficult one. She felt guilty about accepting their protection—room, board, and clothing—while flouting her sister's authority and involving her brother-in-law in the squabbling. She tried to hold her tongue, but she was naturally outspoken, particularly when she felt herself to be attacked unfairly. By the end of her first year with the Korngolds, she was so actively unhappy with Shana's bossiness that very little additional fussing was necessary to trigger an explosion between them.

It happened at the dinner table one evening, and in later years neither Shana nor Golda would be able to recall precisely what this quarrel was about except that, undoubtedly, it was over something quite trivial.

"I'm not a baby," Golda shouted. "You've no right to boss me around as though I were. What have I done wrong? Can you point to one single thing? I don't want to stay here anymore. I'm leaving."

Shana's cheeks were as red as her hair. "Then leave!"

Golda left that evening, taking with her only the few belongings she had brought from Milwaukee, for she could not now accept anything that Shana had provided. It was a costly decision, but, characteristically, once having made it, Golda did not waste time pondering over it or regretting it.

She fled to a temporary haven with a young tubercular couple she knew who lived in a furnished room with an alcove. The most painful part of her predicament was that she would have to drop out of high school in order to support herself. Within a few days Golda found work in a laundry specializing in doing up the lace curtains that were then an almost mandatory status symbol among America's genteel middle- and upper-class families. First she had to stretch the curtain onto a wooden frame and using small, sharp tacks, pin it taut, sizing it to its original length and width. It was extremely onerous work, requiring no special skill but a great deal of patience. At the end of a day's work her fingertips were sore and bleeding. But with her first week's wages she was able to rent a small, cheap furnished room of her own.

Every penny counted if she was to make a go of things. She walked wherever she could in order to save the fare and learned how to eat as thriftily as possible without actually going hungry. Fairly soon, she found another job where the hours were as long—the standard nine-hour day—and the pay as meager, but the work was easier. She was once again employed in a department store, where she sold suit and coat linings and took measurements for made-to-order skirts.

She now began to see a great deal of a young man, Moshe Meyerson, whom she had met a few months before. Moshe was as penniless as she was, since his earnings as a sign painter barely stretched to cover the needs of both himself and his mother, whom he supported. But Moshe was largely indifferent to the material things of life. He was a perpetual dreamer who persistently, even if rather vaguely, sought after the spiritual life. Moshe substituted introspection for action, and like a character out of the works of Chekhov, whom he much admired, he was given to a kind of poetic melancholy—a sweet sadness and pervasive gentleness.

Physically as well as mentally, he was in sharp contrast to Golda. He was some five years older than she and rather short for a man. He had a slight body susceptible to illness and soft, rather nondescript features except for large, kind eyes which gleamed sympathetically from behind his spectacles. Golda was tall, full-bodied, and robust. Her strong, attractive features made her face one to be remembered. Whereas Moshe's personality was quiet and recessive, Golda had great personal magnetism and the ability to communicate instantly with nearly anyone.

Especially since she had dropped out of school, Golda felt strongly that it was important to educate herself on her own. In Moshe she had the perfect teacher. He had read widely, and now he opened up the world of literature to her. He compiled long reading lists for her and sent her exploring channels that she would probably not otherwise have discovered. The Romantic poets especially appealed to Moshe, and he introduced Golda to Lord Byron, William Wordsworth, John Keats, and Percy Bysshe Shelley. Music was second to literature to Moshe, and the couple attended concerts together, broadening and cultivating Golda's musical taste far beyond the Russian and Yiddish songs she had heard at home. Whether or not he could spare the money, Moshe brought her flowers, which helped to brighten her drab little room. Altogether, he was protective, sheltering, understanding, and, as Golda wrote to Regina, "he has a beautiful soul."

"I think," Regina wrote back, "you're beginning to fall in love."

Golda did not deny it.

She had continued to correspond with her mother, who answered her letters, though her father refused to write. Golda maintained the fiction that she was still living with the Korngolds. She was too proud to tell her parents that she was living alone in a miserable little room and working in a department store. Not that Golda looked upon her job as degrading or demeaning—no honest work was looked down upon in her group. But she had not run away from home to sell linings and measure women for skirts; she had left to become, eventually, a schoolteacher. Yet she was now even further away from her goal than she would have been if she had remained in Milwaukee and managed to stay on at school.

A proud and independent Golda, mistress of her own destiny
(*Photo: Zionist Archives and Library, New York*)

27

Somehow, Mrs. Mabovitz found out about Golda's circumstances, and she was frantic. When Golda had been on her own for about six months, she received a letter from her father begging her to come home for her mother's sake. She was deeply moved by the letter because she recognized how painful it must have been for her stiff-necked father to break down and offer to mend the breach between them. Wisely, Mr. Mabovitz realized that Golda would never come home if she was expected to back down or compromise with her ideals. He understood his daughter better than that. Come home, he pleaded, and promised that she could go to high school and then become a teacher if that was what she still wanted.

Parting from Moshe was a wrench, but they considered themselves to be engaged now, and Moshe promised he would follow her to Milwaukee.

The reunion with her family was happy. No more fights! No more quarreling at cross-purposes. No attempts to channel her life in the way she did not wish it to go.

"At last," sixteen-year-old Golda Mabovitz exulted, "at last I have my freedom!"

With the roadblocks removed, Golda, vice-president of her class, graduated from high school with honors less than two years after her return from Denver. Then, in 1915, she enrolled in the Milwaukee Normal School for the teacher-training course.

CHAPTER 4

It's Difficult to Be a Jew

GOLDA FOUND WORLD events in 1915 infinitely more absorbing and challenging than courses in the history of education and pedagogy. With the outbreak of World War I savage pogroms were reported all over eastern Europe. In Poland, Russia, Galicia, and Romania, wherever German armies advanced, Jewish communities were being slaughtered or deported *en masse*. Golda's memories of Cossack brutalities were rekindled when she learned that in Pinsk Jews were lined up and shot against the wall of a church she used to pass by as a child.

Again, Golda spoke up, this time to raise funds for the Jewish People's Relief for Eastern European Jewry. She made speeches at street corners and at meetings in hired halls with such passionate sincerity and depth of conviction that she swept her audiences with her.

"Mustn't we pay something for the fact that we're in America and not with the massacred, downtrodden Jews of the Ukraine?" she demanded. "Will you be able to escape your conscience when it asks what you are doing to show your relationship to the great people perishing in blood across the sea?"

Yet even as she helped to raise money for the relief of persecuted Jews abroad, the question of how to be a Jew without tension and fear became acute for her. She recalled a play, *It's Difficult to Be a Jew*, by the great Yiddish writer Shalom Aleichem. The play opens with a group of children chanting the title. Suddenly, they stop, throw out their hands, and ask with mock seriousness: "Why?" When Golda saw a performance, she had burst out laughing like the rest of the audience, and like the rest of the audience, her laughter had been bitter.

Certainly Jews were not greatly oppressed in America, but even there, as in all the areas of the world to which they had been dispersed, Jews lived as a minority. In not-so-subtle ways they were discriminated against in jobs, housing, hotels and resorts, colleges and graduate schools. Compared to pogroms and mass deportations, these were "small" disadvantages, but, nevertheless, they made being a Jew a liability.

Also, there were disturbing signs that anti-Semitism in America was becoming stronger and more pervasive. In earlier decades the majority of immigrants had been English, Scotch, Irish, and German, and they had contributed to the proud American boast of a melting pot by divesting themselves of their native languages, culture, and customs just as quickly as possible to become "assimilated" into "native" American stock. But increasingly after the turn of the century, when immigrants from eastern Europe like Golda and her family numbered into the hundreds of thousands, they were regarded with hostility and contempt.

"Native" American ears were jarred by the hybrid Yiddish of Russians and Poles; their complexions, stature, dress, and customs were also obviously "different" and thus inferior. Also, predominantly Protestant America looked upon their poverty, cultural level, and alien mentality as a threat to America's standard of living.

Many Americans grumbled: "This country is supposed to be the world's melting pot. If the Jews won't melt, they don't belong."

In 1914, as World War I put an end to mass immigration,

prejudiced Americans began to lobby for the exclusion of foreigners, particularly Jews. Soon after, Congress considered a literacy test for immigrants, which, of course, was intended to exclude those who could neither read nor write English. Since Russian and Polish Jews had been largely restricted to ghetto schools, where only Yiddish or Hebrew was taught, the requirement of having to pass a literacy test would operate to shut them out almost entirely.

This growing climate of exclusionary, restrictive attitudes and measures led Golda to a searching self-examination. Was coming to the aid of persecuted Jews abroad by raising money to rehabilitate them, thereby helping the uprooted to sink new roots in still another hostile, alien land, the best answer to the Jewish question? Golda thought not. Why, instead, should not the Jewish people have the right to one spot on earth where they could live, not by sufferance of others, but as a free, independent people wholly responsible for themselves and their own welfare and safety? Were Zionists who had chosen the never-forgotten ancient homeland of Palestine as the place to build a Jewish nation merely visionaries and dreamers? Even if they were, what was wrong with dreaming?

Besides, as Golda well knew, Zionists had already embarked on a program of action. From the 1880's on, small societies of Jewish pioneers from eastern Europe, called Lovers of Zion, had begun to create settlements in Palestine. They had no practical skills or capital to invest in the barren land, largely desert to the south and malarial swamps to the north. Many of these first settlers died of swamp fever or exhaustion. Perhaps all would have perished had it not been for the financial support of the French Jewish bankers and philanthropists Baron Moritz Hirsch and Baron Edmond de Rothschild. But with their help the settlers founded the first Jewish farm-villages in modern history, giving them such inspiring Hebrew names as

Rishon-le-Zion (First in Zion), Petah Tikvah (Gateway of Hope), and Zichron Yaacov (Memory of Jacob).

And then, in 1897, with the founding of the World Zionist Organization by Theodor Herzl, an Austrian writer, the establishment of a Jewish Home in Palestine became an international movement.

In 1906 a second Aliyah, or immigration, of some forty thousand young Russian men and women brought new strength and vigor to the ancient land. Palestine was then a sorely neglected province of a dying Ottoman Empire. The Arab peasant farmers, fellahin, were virtually feudal serfs to the great Arab landowners and barely managed to keep themselves alive through primitive farming methods unchanged since biblical times. To these fellahin the Jewish settlers were intruders to be met with suspicion, hostility, and acts of violence.

Despite overwhelming obstacles, the members of the second Aliyah were succeeding. Not only were they settling the land, but they were also reviving the Hebrew language and literature; forming a militia, the Shomrim, to safeguard Jewish lives and property by force of arms if necessary; and preparing for coming generations by building a Hebrew high school at Hertseliya, a technical academy at Haifa, and even, in 1913, projecting plans for a great Hebrew university. But they were still pitifully few in numbers and resources, and the World Zionist Organization issued a powerful call to Jews everywhere to make a third Aliyah to Palestine.

To Golda this summons was irresistible. She would go to Palestine because dreams and talk without action were worthless, and if you believed in Zionism as the answer to the question of how to be a Jew without fear, then how could you *not* go? The year was 1915. At the age of seventeen Golda Mabovitz dedicated herself to a vision of a reborn people in a reborn land, and she felt that her life would be meaningful only in the measure that she helped to realize that vision.

Her decision had nothing to do with any sense of disillusion or dissatisfaction with America. On the contrary, as she made clear to her family and to friends who hesitated to make a similar commitment, she felt she had done well here. The boundless opportunities of America were largely open to her. She had the promise of success in her chosen work as a teacher, and her personal relationships were warm and happy. Actually, it was the free climate of America that encouraged her to live according to her beliefs and lent her the strength to do so.

Significantly, she had not up to this point joined any Zionist organization. She had gone to Zionist meetings and studied the literature, but only after she had convinced herself that Zionism held the answer for her, personally, did she become a member of Poalei Zion, which embodied the principles of socialist Zionism.

The brochures of the Poalei Zion quoted the saying of Hillel, the sage, as its own rationale:

> If I am not for myself, who will be for me?
> But if I am for myself only, what am I?
> And if not now, when?

Her fiancé, Moshe Meyerson, responded cautiously to Golda's announcement of her decision to emigrate to Palestine. No Zionist himself, he knew that high-spirited, independent Golda would not take kindly to any restraints he might seek to impose on her. The very idea of emigrating was appalling to Moshe. Reports of the hardships, privations, and dangers of life in Palestine, which only served to stir Golda's blood, depressed and disheartened him. He was not a pioneer. He looked forward to a quiet homelife, children, a few books and phonograph records, and enough

At a Shavuot picnic with other young Milwaukee Zionists, Golda wears a traditional floral wreath in her hair.

leisure to philosophize about a world he felt was beyond his poor powers to change. He told himself that Golda was, after all, very young, still a schoolgirl. She had so much warmth and tenderness in her, such compassion, that naturally she was being swayed by all the Utopian strivings of the Zionists. Soon, he expected to be able to join Golda in Milwaukee and earn a living. Once he was there he might be able to influence her, not against activities in behalf of Zionism, but against leaving the country.

Shana, with whom Golda had long since made up their quarrel, was also filled with misgivings over Golda's decision, but, like Moshe, she now knew better than to take a hard line.

"Golda," she wrote, "don't you think that there is a middle field for idealism right here on the spot?"

Even Regina refrained from pressing Golda. Though sympathetic to Zionism, she was not prepared to commit herself all the way. She felt that when Golda had set the date to leave, it would be time enough for her to reach a decision about joining her.

Totally incapable of doing anything halfheartedly, Golda threw herself into the work of Poalei Zion and soon came under the influence of its grand old man, Nachman Syrkin, whose credo she accepted as her own.

"The Jewish State," he had written, "can come into being only if it is socialist; only by fusing with socialism can Zionism become the ideal of the whole Jewish people."

Another man who deeply impressed her was the fiery Zionist speaker Shmarya Levin, whom she heard castigate the sizable Jewish population of Milwaukee for its lack of vision, disinterest in organized action, and lack of self-assertion—all cardinal sins in her book, too.

But by far the most exciting event was the arrival in Milwaukee of David Ben-Gurion, then aged thirty, a short, stocky, dynamic man, and tall, thin, scholarly Itzhak Ben-Zvi. Both men had been members of the second Aliyah, and both had been exiled from Palestine by the Turkish Government after a short term in jail for "Zionist conspiracy."

Ben-Gurion delivered a simple, bold message to American Jews: Come to us in Palestine and help us settle the land with your own labor. He described how Jewish society was being restructured there by giving Jews the chance to earn a right to the land by their own sweat and toil. For centuries, especially in eastern Europe, Jews had not been allowed to own land; instead they were herded into ghettos in towns and cities and turned their hands to various crafts and shopkeeping. Now the principle of *avodah atsmit* —self-labor—would protect Jews from the indignities and humiliations that had been heaped upon them. Zionism, he proclaimed, was the greatest movement for liberation in human history.

"Don't you see," Golda told Moshe, who had recently arrived in Milwaukee, "it would have been too easy for a small number of Jews to come to Palestine, buy orange groves, and let Arabs work them. Arab labor is cheaper than Jewish labor, and they have no fancy ideas about an eight-hour day. It would have been simple to have Arab workers and Jewish landlords. But if this were allowed to happen, Jews would have no right to return to a land reclaimed through the toil of others."

But Moshe continued to be unimpressed. He had neither the taste nor the muscles for hard self-labor.

Meanwhile, Golda was trying to discover what purpose, if any, was being served by continuing with her courses at normal school. She was not going to teach in Milwaukee. Instead, she was going to Palestine to work the land. The courses were interesting enough, but they had no relevance to the life she was planning to live. Then why not put her time and energy into more immediately useful purposes? True, she must have a job in order to make and save money for the move to Palestine, but a shorter course in library work would do the trick. Also, while training as a librarian, she could teach in the Yiddish Folk School, which the Labor Zionists had established for children to attend after school hours. The matter was settled. Nor did she feel apologetic for having given up the career that had been so vitally important to her a few years before. The future she now planned for herself made regrets or apologies quite unnecessary.

Then, on November 2, 1917, an event occurred that inspired Jewish communities everywhere with new hope and joy. At last the British Government issued the Balfour Declaration, giving official backing to the Zionist aim!

Largely responsible for the event was Dr. Chaim Weizmann, the young man from Pinsk, who had become a brilliant chemist and professor at the University of Manchester in England. His discovery of a new process for making acetone, a chemical essential to the production of cordite (gunpowder) had been vital to the British war effort. Rejecting honors for himself, Weizmann had requested help from the Government in returning Jews to their homeland in Palestine.

Lord Arthur Balfour, the Foreign Secretary, granted the request in the form of a letter to the British Jewish leader, Baron Rothschild, of the Zionist Federation in London:

> His Majesty's Government view with favour the establishment in Palestine of a National Home for the Jewish people, and will use their best endeavours to facilitate the achievement of this objective, it being clearly understood that nothing shall be done that shall prejudice the civil and religious rights of existing non-Jewish communities in Palestine, or the rights and political status enjoyed by Jews in any other country.

It was not open sesame to the land, but, Golda thought, her eyes filling, it was more than enough for her and for others, who were like-minded and like-hearted, to make a beginning.

CHAPTER 5

Palestine: The Naked Land

M

OSHE

M

EYERSON

HAD

 finally to face up to the fact that
Golda would never change her mind about going to Palestine and that unless he promised to emigrate with her, their
engagement would be called off.

She was deeply drawn to him by his qualities of gentleness and kindliness, and she appreciated how greatly he
had contributed to her growth. But she would not—indeed,
could not, even if she had wished—settle for a life of conventional domesticity. She was an activist, a doer. Though
she looked forward to being a good wife and mother, it
would be after her own fashion, which meant that she did
not propose to serve the needs of her family exclusively. It
seemed to her that to settle on a kibbutz in Palestine offered a perfect solution. First, a kibbutz was a voluntary
collective farm community which came closest to carrying
out the ideals of socialist Zionism; and second, life was so
arranged on a kibbutz that she could pioneer on the land
while being relieved of most domestic chores and of much
of the burden of child-rearing.

Moshe disliked the idea of living in Palestine as much as
ever, and he was still unconvinced that Zionism was the
answer to Jewish problems. But he loved Golda with all his
being, and her ultimatum, in effect, left him no other choice.
He accepted its terms and asked only that they marry at

once, for there was no reason whatever to wait any longer.

On December 24, 1917, Golda and Moshe were married in a Milwaukee synagogue. Included in their marriage vows before the rabbi was the promise that they would both go to Palestine to live. Now, certainly, there could be no turning back!

Moshe continued to earn a modest living by sign-painting. He was not at all unhappy that their departure for Palestine had been delayed, because all transatlantic passenger service had been canceled for the duration of the war. But some months before the Balfour Declaration, Britain had at last agreed to the formation of a Jewish Legion, which would assist in the fight for the liberation of Palestine from the Turks. David Ben-Gurion and Itzhak Ben-Zvi ended their exile by returning to Palestine with the legion, and when the United States entered the war, many young American Labor Zionists were also permitted to enlist in it, fighting their way into the country in order to settle there. Golda grasped at this possibility of reaching Palestine sooner. She asked to enlist in the legion and to serve in any capacity, but she was turned down because no women were being accepted.

"Volunteers for the Jewish Legion left from our home, each with a small bag that Mama sewed filled with goodies," Golda wrote Regina, who was then working as a secretary in Chicago. "But," she added sadly, "we had to wait."

Nachman Syrkin and other leaders of the Poalei Zion recognized what a treasure they had in Golda Meyerson, a young, extremely dynamic woman, who could speak brilliantly and fluently in both English and Yiddish and who had a gift for recruiting and organizing. They offered her a full-time job with Poalei Zion, traveling about the country to organize party branches. Her pay would be fifteen dollars a week and expenses, which was even less than the low salaries then paid to teachers and librarians. But Golda eagerly accepted. What a wonderful break to be able to do what she most wanted to do—and be paid for it!

The job meant frequent absences from home, but Moshe made no serious objection, contenting himself with Golda's letters, which were often written hurriedly but always with affection and full of wifely advice about taking good care of himself.

By 1918, at the age of twenty, Golda had made such an outstanding reputation that despite her youth, she was appointed one of Poalei Zion's delegates to the first meeting of the American Jewish Congress, which, in turn, was to select delegates to the Versailles Peace Conference. At Versailles the Balfour Declaration was to be officially approved, and Britain was to be designated as trustee of the Palestine Mandate.

For the first time Golda was among some of the most highly placed, wealthy, and influential Jews in America, as well as in the more familiar company of labor unionists and Zionists. When her hero, Nachman Syrkin, was chosen to be among the representatives to the peace conference, her cup of joy, already filled to the brim, spilled over.

"I tell you," she wrote Moshe, "that some moments reached such heights that after them one could have died happy!"

The end of the war removed the last obstacle to sailing for Palestine—all except raising the money for passage for themselves and their household goods.

The time had come for Regina Hamburger to decide whether she would go to Palestine with her dearest Golda. After consulting with her fiancé, Yossel Kopelov, she agreed to join Golda and the other members of the Aliyah, "out of romanticism," she said candidly, "out of an appetite for high adventure, and also out of conviction."

The Meyersons, Regina and Yossel, and another couple pooled their savings and made the first leg of their long journey from Milwaukee to New York City, where they rented a large apartment in Morningside Heights which they shared communally. From September, 1920, to May, 1921, they were all working industriously to raise money for their passage: Moshe painted signs, Yossel became a barber, Regina did secretarial work in the office of the *Menorah Journal*, and Golda continued to do tasks for Poalei Zion while also working in a branch of the New York Public Library.

The Korngolds, who now had two young children, had not considered joining the Aliyah. But when Golda visited them to say good-bye, Sam turned to Shana and said teasingly, "Perhaps you'd like to go, too?" And to everyone's amazement Shana replied, "Yes, if you give me money for expenses." Just what impulse accounted for her behavior, even Shana herself was not quite sure. She loved Sam deeply, yet she was proposing to separate from him. How long the separation would last neither of them could tell, for Sam would be supporting his wife and children in Palestine, and only when he had accumulated a surplus, would he be able to join them. Later, Shana recognized that her secret revolutionary activity as a teen-ager and her yearnings toward Zionism as a young wife and mother had motivated her. To go to Palestine meant putting herself where her mind and heart directed her to go—just as Golda had concluded much earlier.

Passage was arranged on the S.S. *Pocahontas*, which was to take them and a party of twenty-two other young Americans to Naples and via Egypt to Palestine. Departure was set for May 23, 1921.

But on May 1 reports reached the United States of another outbreak, one of a long series, of Arab riots at the seaport of Jaffa, which rapidly spread throughout Palestine. Much property was damaged and destroyed, and some four hundred persons, about equally divided between Jews and

Arabs, were killed or injured. The families and friends of the young emigrants pleaded with them to delay their sailing or not to go at all. On schedule, though, the small company of American Zionist pioneers boarded ship.

This embarkation was about the only thing that did go off on schedule!

Golda's own account reveals that nearly everything that could go wrong, did, during that endless voyage:

"It had taken us three years to obtain money for tickets, but finally the day arrived—May 23, 1921—when we boarded a small, decrepit ship bound for Naples, the first leg on our way to Palestine. We were a small group, young, full of hope and zeal, ready for anything. We were all looking forward to the wonderful prospect of an ocean voyage, but right from the start it turned into a nightmare. First, we couldn't sail because of a strike. Then we spent nine days in Boston harbor, and our Zionist friends came up from New York and kissed us good-bye every day. The crew, still in a strike mood, had mutinied, and the engines broke down. Many of our group left us in Boston, but the rest of us were not to be put off by mutinies or sabotaged machinery.

"After we put to sea, supposedly repaired and shipshape, new troubles hit us. Pumps and boilers broke down, and the condensers and refrigerators followed suit. Food spoiled and had to be thrown overboard, leaving only bully beef and brackish water for the passengers. Fire broke out in two of the holds. The engine room flooded. Several of the crew were put in irons.

"We huddled in our cabins till we put in at the Azores for repairs. Four engineers went ashore boasting that they were going to sink the ship before it reached Naples. The captain heard about this and clapped them in irons, too."

In the Azores the Jewish community learned about the poor, bedeviled passengers, and while the ship was being repaired, they wined and dined the young Americans until their money ran out and the young people had to fend for themselves. When they went to a restaurant and saw the prices were in hundreds of escudos, they were afraid to eat.

"In Naples," Golda continued, "our baggage disappeared. Because of riots and pogroms, no ships would land Jews in Palestine, and we ran out of funds while waiting in Naples. Finally, we found a way to go, with an Egyptian visa by boat to Alexandria and then by train to Palestine."

The voyage had taken fifty-three days. But on July 14, 1921, they reached Palestine!

The British immigration inspector asked Golda, "What in the world do you expect to find to do in Palestine?"

A dozen years later he found himself working under Golda as part of her staff at Histadrut, the labor federation.

She never forgot her first impression of Palestine:

"It was discouraging. The reality proved to be more difficult—and more wonderful—than even our hardy spirits had anticipated. We knew that we would face an unkind Nature, political hostility, poverty, and personal hardship, but I, for one, did not believe that man should abdicate because the forces opposing him are too mighty."

They had all known the hardships and dislocation of emigrating from Europe to America and settling into a strange land. But in the United States they had a country to settle in, with cities and industries and a government. In Palestine there were no cities, no commerce or industry —nothing but hostile Arabs abetted by a British Mandate Government that pursued a policy of appeasement toward them.

The small Yishuv, as the Jewish community in Palestine was called before statehood, had been wracked by suffering during the war years. Food supplies were at a near-starvation level. Turkish indifference to the plight of the people and nonexistent sanitation or medical care had taken many lives.

Golda was appalled at how the little Arab and Jewish children looked when she first arrived: "Where eyes should have been, no eyes were to be seen. They were covered with flies."

At a school in Jaffa one lone nurse struggled to keep the children's eyes healthy, but trachoma, a highly infectious eye disease, had reached epidemic proportions.

One of the few heartening sights for Golda was the little Hadassah Hospital on the sands in Tel Aviv, built through the valiant efforts of Henrietta Szold, who in 1912 had founded Hadassah, an organization for the promotion of Zionism in America and the establishment of health services in Palestine. It was Hadassah, not the British Mandate officials, that did preventive sanitary work in the immigrant camps and provided each with a sanitary inspector, a nurse, and a doctor.

Although they had a bare minimum to live on, the Meyersons, Shana and her two children, and Regina and Yossel were better off than the immigrants from Europe. Instead of living in a tent, they could afford to rent two rooms in Tel Aviv with an outside kitchen and toilet. There was no running water or electricity. They used kerosene lamps and bought just enough food to last a single day because they did not even have an ice chest. They learned to store a piece of butter or margarine in the clay crocks the Arabs used.

When their lost baggage finally arrived, they pressed their trunks into service as furniture: one trunk, draped with curtain material, became a table; two trunks joined together made a sofa; and another two were transformed into dressers. The men put up shelves for dishes and pots, pictures were hung, and as an elegant touch, one of the packing cases was covered with a cloth to serve as a pedestal for a statue.

The pièce de résistance was Golda and Moshe's phonograph, widely touted as the first modern phonograph without a big horn in all of Palestine. There were also the records that Moshe, who could not live without music, had carefully selected and brought with them. People flocked to their rooms to listen to music and to socialize.

Morale among them varied. Life was hardest on Shana, who had to care for two young children without the comforts and amenities she had grown accustomed to in America. She must also endure the added privation of being separated from her husband.

Yossel, Regina's fiancé, proved to be a great complainer, and Golda, who had a very low opinion of complainers, wrote caustically about him to Sam Korngold: "As soon as we arrived, in fact as we got off the train, Yossel wanted to return at once. Not for political reasons but simply because sitting in America is easier than doing the work. To deny oneself various comforts is also easier in talk than in deed. . . ."

As Yossel went on complaining, Regina lost patience with him and broke off their engagement. She was not enjoying the primitive living conditions or the sand and the flies and said so in a letter to her parents.

Her father wrote: "I guess we'll have to send you fare to come back."

At once, Regina's spine stiffened and she determined to remain. Of them all, she was in the best position to get a good job. The British Mandate had provided for an "appropriate Jewish Agency" to advise and to cooperate with the Palestine Administration in all matters affecting the "establishment of the Jewish National Home." In other words, the Jewish Agency was the official spokesman for the Yishuv and its seat of self-government. As an American girl with typing and stenography skills, Regina was snapped up by the Jewish Agency and started work with them in Jerusalem, thus embarking on a secretarial career which, throughout her life, offered the "romance and high adventure" she had set out to find in Palestine.

Moshe was reasonably content, chiefly because Golda, in-

Kiryath Anavim, a village near Jerusalem

different to hardships, was so radiantly happy. He found odd jobs to do, marking time, until they were admitted to the kibbutz.

For Golda, marking time was exasperating, but she reined her impatience and gave English lessons while she set herself to learning Hebrew, which was the accepted everyday language of the Yishuv. She ached to begin work in the kibbutz and dig into the soil of Palestine. She took her first trip to Jerusalem from Tel Aviv, a trip that in those days took two and a half to three hours to cover a distance of forty miles. The road was dusty, the July heat muggy and oppressive, and on both sides of the road there was nothing but naked rock.

"It was depressing," she wrote a friend in New York, "and yet I was happy that I saw naked rock. You see, some-day when there is a forest along this road, I will know and everybody will know that those trees were not planted for us. Nor did we find them there. The trees will be there because we planted them."

Even before leaving America, Golda had selected Merhavia as the kibbutz she and Moshe would ask to join. She was influenced by the fact that one of their Milwaukee friends, a young man who had joined the Jewish Legion and settled in Palestine after the war, was among a number of Americans there. At this period, kibbutz members took in newcomers around Rosh Hashanah, the Jewish holiday that marked the beginning of a new year. Then everyone had to declare whether or not he was remaining in the kibbutz, for membership was wholly voluntary. Until the number of vacancies was known, new applications could not be acted on. But Rosh Hashanah of 1921 rolled by, and still no decision had been made on the Meyersons' application. Three meetings of the kibbutz general assembly were held before the Meyersons were reluctantly accepted.

Golda learned that she was the reason for this reluctance. Many kibbutz members felt that she, as a "pampered American girl," would not have the stamina to endure the hard physical labor and rough life at Merhavia. In the end Golda became convinced that she and Moshe were accepted because of their phonograph. Since all personal property belonged to the kibbutz, the phonograph became communal property. Even kibbutzniks who lived in almost fanatical austerity, eschewing all luxuries, could not resist listening and dancing to music.

CHAPTER 6

Some of the Happiest Years

THE FIRST KIBBUTZ in Palestine, called Degania ("corn-flower"), was founded in 1909 by a handful of settlers, nine men and women, and it set the pattern for a whole new life-style.

In Hebrew the word "kibbutz" means group or gathering, but it is a very special kind of group: a voluntary collective community based on the principle of cooperative labor to which each person contributes according to his ability and receives according to his need.

No money was used within the kibbutz. Everything—all property, including clothing and home furnishings as well as the land and livestock—was owned in common by kibbutz members. All kibbutzniks were entitled to all community services regardless of the kind of work they performed. No hired labor was permitted. No private trading was tolerated. All marketing and purchasing was done by the group as a whole, and all profits were ploughed back into the further development of the settlement. Total equality of the sexes was basic to the kibbutz idea; men and women must share equally in the work and the benefits derived from their labor.

"Imagine!" Golda cried. "Just imagine living by our own labor in a community where we're all equal, no rich or poor, no snobbery, no exploitation!"

The kibbutz Merhavia was founded in 1911 in the valley

of Jezreel by young pioneers from Russia. But World War I had interrupted its development, and when peace came, the settlement was divided into a kvutzah, or complete cooperative, and a moshav, or settlement in which land was individually owned, but self-labor and cooperative purchase and use of equipment as well as marketing of produce were the rule.

Golda chose the kvutzah because it was undiluted socialism, a purer form of Labor Zionism than the moshav. When she and Moshe arrived at Merhavia, there were prewar frame houses and a primitive shack, which served as a communal kitchen and bakery. The total membership of the kibbutz was only thirty-two, of which all but eight were men. Because of their initial reluctance to accept her into the kibbutz, Golda determined that right from the start she would prove to them how badly they had misjudged the character and stamina of an American girl.

At the time, one of the main sources of income to the kibbutz was the money each member received from the Jewish National Fund for planting trees. The plot of ground was full of rocks and boulders which had to be loosened with picks in order to reach soil in which to plant the saplings. Since most of the girls had at least half a dozen years' experience in the kibbutz, they swung their picks like veterans. Golda asked no quarter. Although she had never handled a pick before, she doggedly kept pace with the rest of the tree-planters.

At a price!

"When I returned to my room in the evening," Golda told friends, "I couldn't so much as move a finger, but I knew that if I didn't show up for supper the others would jeer: 'What did I tell you? That's an American girl for you!' I would gladly have forgone supper, for the chick-pea mush we ate wasn't worth the effort of lifting the fork to my mouth—but I went!"

Each member or married couple was assigned a room

furnished with bed, dresser, and a couple of chairs. No one had a private toilet or shower. Not so much as a cup of coffee could be prepared in one's own room because all the cooking facilities were in the communal kitchen and all food was eaten at long tables in the communal dining room. In the summer the long trek to toilets, shower, or dining hall meant trudging along one of the dusty paths that crisscrossed the kibbutz, and in winter it meant slogging in deep mud in the icy cold. But the kibbutz ideal encouraged Spartan living; otherwise members might withdraw from community life in favor of personal comforts.

Everything connected with food presented problems. The girls alternately drew a month's assignment to kitchen duty, although men also helped out. Whenever their turns came around, the girls complained bitterly, and Golda could not understand why kitchen duty should send them into such a tizzy.

"Why," Golda asked them, "can you go to work cleaning out the barn and feeding the cows without being depressed about it, but you can't feel the same when it's your turn to go to the kitchen to feed our comrades? Why do you regard this work as demeaning?"

What Golda failed to realize was that those girls had been treated like second-class citizens in Europe, with little of the status and rights that American girls took for granted. To them, equality meant equality with men, to work side by side with them clearing the land, planting trees, working in the orchards, driving a tractor. Kitchen work was "women's work," and they despised it because they felt it discriminated against and downgraded them.

The food was extremely monotonous. Humus, or chickpeas, soaked in water for twenty-four hours and then boiled or fried with onions, was fobbed off on the kibbutzniks as either soup, cereal, or salad. Golda was sure that much of this monotony was due to lack of imagination and concern about food, but she enjoyed cooking and baking and saw the kitchen assignment as an opportunity to introduce a few innovations to improve the quality and appearance of the food. She found that baking bread, however, was almost impossible.

"Baking bread," she announced to the old-timer who undertook to teach her, "is for me one of the profoundest mysteries of life!"

The flour, bought from Arabs in Nazareth, was poorly sifted, making it difficult to work with. Finally, the old-timer taught her how to knead the dough when it was almost dry, which was a sticky, difficult technique, but it was a proud day for Golda when she turned out her first edible loaf.

One of the leftovers from the war era was cans of so-called fresh herring—fish preserved in tomato paste—which was served cold for breakfast. The kibbutzniks rarely had more than one utensil each, either a knife or a fork or a spoon, and peeling the herring was a clumsy, messy chore, yet the girls merely washed the herring without removing the skin. Moreover, since such refinements as napkins were absent, they wiped their hands on their work clothes, and the pervading smell in the dining room was right out of the bottom of a herring barrel.

Golda sniffed, wrinkled her nose, and decided to do something about the smell. When her turn in the kitchen came, she took the time and trouble to peel the herring before it was served.

Outraged, the other girls said spitefully: "You'll see! She'll get the kibbutzniks used to being coddled, and then we'll have to peel the herring, too!"

Golda retorted: "What would you have done in your own home? How would you serve herring at your own family table? This is your home! They are your family!"

When, on cold winter mornings, Golda decided that her

comrades needed something hot for breakfast and cooked cereal, the girls were outraged again.

"She'll have us used to eating hot cereal for breakfast, yet!"

And Golda did get them used to it, and they loved it.

Golda tangled with the girls over still other kibbutz practices. Laundry was done communally, but ironing, an arduous business of using heavy irons heated by hot coals, was left to individual choice. All week long, the girls went to work in unironed clothing, but Golda appeared daily in a neatly ironed dress and kerchief.

"What're you so mad about?" Golda demanded of her critics. "What do you care? I do the ironing on my own time, in my own room!"

And then a chance came to demonstrate that in spite of herring-peeling and clothes-ironing, the American girl was no "softie."

Merhavia had a water tower, but frequently, particularly in the summer, when the kibbutzniks, covered with dust from the fields, stepped into the shower and opened the tap, no water flowed out. A very tall ladder had to be climbed to the top of the water tower and an adjustment made with a wrench. When the girls were caught without water, they ran around the kibbutz looking for the handyman to fix it. But when this happened to Golda, she picked up the wrench, climbed the ladder, and made the adjustment herself while the kibbutzniks gathered to stare at her in amazement.

"Why are you so surprised?" Golda asked. "Why should an American girl need a man to fix a little thing like that?"

One of her first assignments was to pick almonds in the orchard, but shortly after her arrival at Merhavia she was sent to a nearby settlement to attend the first course ever given in the country in modern methods of poultry-raising. After completing the course, Golda was put in charge of the poultry at the kibbutz, managing the chicken houses and

Feeding the chickens at Kibbutz Merhavia in 1921

chicken runs and the five-hundred-egg incubator in which the kibbutz had just invested. Up to this point, there had only been a few scrawny chickens, and eggs were classed as luxuries.

But Golda had great success with her chickens. "I feel," she wrote Shana, "as though I was born to be a chicken-breeder!"

The area around the kibbutz was marshy and malaria-ridden, and quinine was served daily at mealtimes. Both she and Moshe had been hospitalized by attacks of malaria, but Golda came down with another disease then prevalent in the country, called *papetache,* a debilitating high fever accompanied by terrible headache and total loss of appetite. While she was in bed with the fever, the kibbutzniks for-

got to water the chickens, and when she recovered sufficiently to attend to them herself, she saw that a number of
them had died of thirst. Her fever shot way up again, and
she had a nightmare in which her room was filled with dead
chickens.

But the bout of fever showed Golda how highly she was
regarded by her comrades. One of the kibbutzniks rode on
horseback to the Arab town of Afula to bring ice and lemons
with which to make lemonade for her. Nothing, she assured
her comrades, would ever taste as exquisite to her as that
cold lemonade!

Merhavia was located between two Arab villages, and the
Arabs used to take potshots at the kibbutzniks from time to
time. Early on, Golda learned never to wear white at night
and make a target of herself. Although she was certain the
day would come when there would be no more potshots from
Arabs and no more malaria, she felt there would never be
an end to the *barhash,* an infestation of tiny flies during
the barley season.

Even years later, she vividly recalled what a plague those
pesky flies were:

"In the summer we went out to work at four in the morning, for when the sun came up, it was impossible to stay in
the field for the *barhash.* We used to smear ourselves with
Vaseline (when we had it), wear high collars and long
sleeves, wrap ourselves in kerchiefs, and come home with
the *barhash* stuck in our eyes, ears, and nostrils. Even the
cows used to stampede from the fields when the *barhash*
came out. I had a solution for all my other problems, but
not the *barhash.*"

Besides her work in the chicken houses, Golda's old sideline of giving English lessons proved a valuable asset to the
kibbutz. A grocer in a nearby village, who came from Germany, sent his daughter to Golda for English lessons, which
she gave after her regular working hours. Instead of cash

payment, the grocer gave the kibbutz a monthly credit at his store, providing such luxuries as potatoes, lemons, "Kwoker" (Quaker Oats), salt, and even raisins for the flour-and-water cookies that were a kibbutz staple.

One day, as a result of the kibbutzniks' labors, the valley of Jezreel would be covered with lush orchards, but there was then no fruit except for those treasured medicinal lemons. Every now and then, Golda visited Shana in Tel Aviv, a trip that involved an overnight stay in Haifa. One of these visits coincided with the height of the citrus season there, and Golda bought a sack of oranges for the kibbutz. The problem was how to lug the large heavy sack to the station and then all the way to the kibbutz from the junction at Afula. It did not occur to Golda to hire a porter, for to walk empty-handed while someone else carried the sack for her was an unthinkable breach of self-labor. Instead, heaving and puffing, Golda shouldered the sack and staggered into Merhavia with it. The kibbutzniks were overjoyed, for which Golda was happy, but, oh, her aching back!

Acts of generosity like these would not have of themselves earned the favor of the kibbutz. Success at work was the only passport to acceptance, and Golda's credentials were a match for anyone else's. Within a year of her arrival at Merhavia her comrades appointed her as their delegate to the recently formed labor federation Histadrut, which acted as coordinator of the various kibbutzim, industries, and trade unions in Palestine. Also, as a mark of unusual regard, Golda was permitted to speak Yiddish at meetings, although Hebrew, in which she was not yet sufficiently proficient, was mandatory for everyone else.

Golda accepted everything about kibbutz life: its combination of idealism and practicality; its high-mindedness and selflessness on most issues yet its narrow and often absurd prejudices on others. Above all, each sapling she planted, each almond she picked, and each chicken she raised filled her with happiness and pride that the work of her own hands was helping to build a Jewish homeland.

For Moshe, life at Merhavia was a totally different kind of experience. He did the chores assigned to him dutifully but with only moderate success, because most of the labor demanded more of him physically than he had to give. Moreover, he was simply unable to believe that what he was being called upon to do and sacrifice held any long-range significance either for himself or for Zionism. The attacks of malaria further debilitated him. But what he minded most of all was the absence of personal privacy. Evenings were spent in some form of communal activity, such as planning sessions of the general assembly or committee meetings on special projects. Festive occasions, when everyone danced the hora until ready to collapse, were also repugnant to him.

One source of self-expression for Moshe was the letters he wrote his mother in America, describing his frustration and unhappiness. In turn, she pressed Moshe and Golda more and more urgently to return. Golda brushed these pleading letters aside and at first refused even to discuss returning to the United States. As Moshe's spirits and energies waned, Golda's waxed, and a clash between them was inevitable.

As time went on, Moshe's misery began to depress even Golda's high spirits and move her to compassion. Poor Moshe! He had yielded to her wishes in everything, but his needs and desires had been largely ignored. If only he could take heart in what they were doing here, if only he could whip up a little enthusiasm for the great undertaking in Palestine, if only . . . But Golda knew that all the if onlys were merely empty, fruitless, wishful thinking. The reality was that Moshe was himself and she was herself. Neither of them was better or more worthy than the other. They were different but surely two people who had made sacred marriage vows and had already shared six years of their lives together should be able to find some way out of the impasse.

With people of goodwill and good faith, Golda believed, all things were negotiable. And so Golda and Moshe negotiated a compromise: They would leave the kibbutz but remain in Palestine. Two and a half years in Merhavia had been a pitifully short time, yet they had been, and would remain, among the happiest years of her life.

CHAPTER 7

"For Such a Woman There Is No Rest"

THE DECISION TO leave Merhavia was bitter medicine to Golda, and she knew that she would never altogether succeed in ridding herself of the aftertaste, but what could be more futile and self-defeating than to dwell on it? The important thing to consider was that on or off a kibbutz she was still in Palestine and could make a contribution.

She and Moshe moved to Tel Aviv, where they both found jobs, she as a cashier and Moshe as a bookkeeper, in the office of Solel Boneh, Histadrut's contracting and public-works enterprise. Within the year, Golda became pregnant, and although she was extremely happy at the prospect of bearing a child, and especially a sabra ("fruit of the cactus," as a child born in Palestine was called), motherhood meant giving up her job. Moshe was jubilant! Perhaps, as he still liked to believe, being a mother would make Golda content with the domesticity he yearned for.

Moshe had been unwilling to have children while they remained in the kibbutz. He did not want his offspring to be a piece of community property, as he viewed it, who would be taken care of by whichever kibbutznik was assigned to the nursery and who would not even sleep under its parents' roof. He could not accept the principle that if the kibbutz were to survive, all babies must be cared for in the children's house by one *metapelet*, or substitute mother, in order to release the other mothers for full-time work. Equally important to the survival of the kibbutz was that children be trained to communal living from infancy onward, absorbing the social and moral values of kibbutz life so that they would preserve and transmit them.

They moved to Jerusalem, where their first child, a son, was born in November, 1924. Once again, Moshe failed to gauge the depth of Golda's determination to be a wife and mother yet take an active role in building a Jewish homeland. Once again they were in conflict, and Golda persuaded Moshe to accept another compromise: that she return to Merhavia with her son, Menahem, and at least give motherhood on a kibbutz a fair trial.

When Menahem was four months old, Golda went to the kibbutz, where three other babies had been born during her absence. One of the girls was detailed as a night nurse, or watchman, at the children's house, and Golda suggested that she relieve the kibbutzniks of this assignment by having her own and the other babies sleep in with her.

"In Jerusalem I became used to getting up during the night when Menahem cried," she said. "So why shouldn't I also get up for the others?"

Her living quarters consisted of two rooms; she put all four babies in the larger of the two, and she slept in the small one. The experiment worked out well except that there was only one bathtub for all the babies, and Golda's passion for cleanliness asserted itself. Soon word got around in the kibbutz that "Golda's babies drink alcohol."

Golda laughed with the others but fought the good fight and won her point. "I slosh alcohol around the bathtub after each baby's turn and 'burn it out' to make sure it is sterile," she explained. "I know this is quite an expense, but I'm sure it is necessary, and I will continue to sterilize the bathtub after each baby's bath."

Moshe responded to Golda's experimental motherhood in

Merhavia with letters begging her to return to Jerusalem and live a normal life. Perhaps not so oddly, Golda, who could remain adamant over an issue like sterilizing a baby's bathtub or, on another level, refuse to budge on a matter of moral principle, was incapable of bringing clearheaded logic or firm resolution to bear in dealing with her husband. Her feelings toward him were confused; her deep sense of loyalty and the duty she owed him were compounded by feelings of guilt. She had been the one to deliver the ultimatum demanding that Moshe accompany her to Palestine as the price he must pay for marriage. And, obviously, Moshe was paying a very steep price for his consent. In the kibbutz his always precarious health had been undermined. Off the kibbutz, in Tel Aviv, which was a pioneer settlement built on sand, and in Jerusalem, built on naked rock, Moshe continued to feel uprooted and alienated from his environment. Nor was his mother helping to boost his morale. She continued to write urgent letters, asking him to come home with or without his wife and offering to pay his passage. Yet he clung to Golda. It was inconceivable to him to separate from her.

Those closest to her, Shana and Regina and other intimates, understood, better than Golda did, the source of her confusion. For all her activism and strength, Golda was a deeply sentimental woman, easily moved by another's distress. Where Moshe was concerned, she could not be objective. His dependency on her, his gentleness and sensitivity made it impossible for her to break away from him. So, after six months on the kibbutz, she returned to Jerusalem, her mind made up to do her utmost to be simply a housewife, to cut herself off from everything else, and to interest herself in nothing outside her family.

Their two-room flat in a shabby suburb of Jerusalem near Mea Shearim had neither gas nor electricity. They used kerosene both for lighting and for the cooking, which was done in a tin shack in the yard. They improvised furniture from orange crates and whatever they could scrounge cheaply in the Arab bazaars. Moshe's wages were meager, even by the prevailing low standards, and he was paid in credit slips rather than money. The local grocer accepted the chits at a discount, but the landlord believed that "in God we trust, all others pay cash."

In 1926 Golda gave birth to a daughter, Sara, and the struggle became rougher than ever. In exchange for Menahem's tuition at a nursery school, Golda took in its laundry, heating water pail by pail and scrubbing piece by piece over a washboard. The children were always down with colds and sore throats, for an unheated apartment during Jerusalem's cold, sleety winters was an ordeal for the hardiest.

After some months as a laundress, Golda's old standby, giving English lessons, came to her rescue, and with baby Sara under her arm she taught at a private school. But debts to the grocer and landlord continued to pile up, and the Meyersons might have sunk had it not been for sister Shana, who sent "wholesale" vegetables from Tel Aviv, and friends like Regina, who was married to a comparatively prosperous journalist, Moshe Medzini. Also, Golda's parents, who had emigrated to Palestine the year Sara was born, were well off by current standards with the land they had purchased in Hertseliya, and they helped out, too.

Golda was immersed in caring for her babies, hunting food bargains, and housecleaning the dingy rooms. What troubled her most was not their acute poverty but her feeling that she was contributing nothing toward the goals that had been her reason for coming to Palestine.

"There is a type of woman who cannot remain at home," she said, explaining her dilemma. "In spite of the place her children and family fill in her life, her nature demands something more; she cannot divorce herself from the larger

Golda, a wife and mother now in her early thirties, emerges into public life.

social life. She cannot let her children narrow her horizon. For such a woman there is no rest."

At the end of four years, which had been the most burdensome of her life, Golda decided to become active in the affairs of the country. She was painfully aware of how dearly she must pay for the decision: "A mother is a mother, and I had to be away from my children very often. Certainly there was conflict. I know what a woman who devotes herself, as I did, to her country has to give up. Someone else brings up her children; the baby's first smile is reserved for someone else. Yes, it's impossible to have everything; you have to pay the price."

The political party to which Golda belonged was the Achdut Haavoda, the Labor party soon to broaden its base to become the Mapai. Friends in the party, eager to see her emerge from domestic life, helped her secure an appointment as secretary of Moetzot Hapoalot, the Women's Labor Council of Histadrut. Its members were young women from Jewish middle-class families in Europe who had come to Palestine to help create a new social order with guarantees of full emancipation and equality for women. Few of them had any training in agriculture or, for that matter, in any of the skills needed for the evolution of the new society. Golda's task was to help establish training farms for the girls and such backup communal facilities as nurseries and kindergartens for the children of working women. Later that year Golda was sent to the United States as an emissary to Pioneer Women, the American counterpart of Moetzot Hapoalot, to coordinate activities there and in Palestine.

She returned to Palestine in the summer of 1929 just as Arab riots turned into murderous attacks on Jews in the Old City of Jerusalem. The center of agitation was the Wailing Wall, which was Moslem property but by long-established custom was accessible to Jews for worship. Despite all hopes of peaceful coexistence, it became apparent that the two nationalities, Jewish and Arab, were in basic, head-on conflict.

Underlying the conflict was the British Mandate's policy of appeasing the Arabs, a policy that it felt served the best interest of the Empire. After all, the Middle East was occupied by a massive Arab population. The Jews were a powerless and relatively unimportant minority; moreover, they were stiff-necked, independent, and proud and refused to behave like a subordinate people.

Ironically, the head of the Mandate Government was a Jew, Sir Herbert Samuel, who, proving how impartial he was, had appointed Amin el-Husseini, a militant Jew-hater, as mufti of Jerusalem and, later, president of the Supreme Moslem Council. By ceaseless violent opposition the mufti hoped to achieve three goals: the revocation of the Balfour Declaration, the establishment of an Arab state in Palestine, and the gradual erosion of the Jewish National Home until it ceased to exist altogether.

The Yishuv answer to Arab violence was to broaden the membership and activities of the Shomrim, the guards at the kibbutzim and settlements, into an underground defense army, the Haganah. Golda enrolled as a member at once. Again she remembered the sound of hammers nailing boards to the windows of her home in Kiev and the feeling of helplessness. Now it was to be quite different! Her children and grandchildren would never know what it meant to be defenseless against danger. They would know how to defend themselves. They would not have bare hands.

Except for a small cadre of full-time staff officers and instructors, the Haganah was made up of civilians of both sexes—farmers, workers, students, professionals, and clerks. Since the Jews were forbidden to carry arms by the terms of the Mandate, the Haganah had to train secretly at night or over weekends learning to handle firearms and to become experts at concealing weapons and keeping its units together by a system of couriers, much as American Minutemen operated in prerevolutionary days. Whenever Arabs attacked, Haganah members protected Jewish villages, settlements, and road traffic.

The 1929 Arab riots had aroused sharp and bitter debate as to the merits of the Jewish "case" versus the Arab "case" within and without the ranks of world labor. Because of her work for the Women's Labor Council and her fluency in English, Golda was named to represent the Palestine Labor Federation at the 1930 Imperial Labor Conference in London. While making a passionate appeal in behalf of Jewish workers, she came to the special attention of David Ben-Gurion, head of the Jewish Agency, and from then on, Golda Meyerson, at the age of thirty-two, was launched as a new political force in Palestine.

First, though, she must undergo more basic training, and in 1932, accompanied by eight-year-old Menahem and six-year-old Sara, she left for a two-year assignment in the United States as National Secretary of Pioneer Women.

Her task was to broaden the membership of Pioneer Women by bringing the message of pioneer Palestine to American women and enlisting their help. Also, and not so explicitly defined, her work was to involve a good deal of political infighting among those American Zionists who felt that American-style capitalism and free competition, not labor socialism, would best serve the interests of Jews in Palestine. Another of her tasks was to edit the *Pioneer Women's Journal,* and this was a burden to her, since she had no special aptitude for writing and could never command the spontaneity and eloquence of her speaking style.

As always, her greatest success was in speaking to groups small or large, whether of old-fashioned, middle-aged women who preferred Golda to speak to them in Yiddish or young women who had been born and college-educated in the United States.

Her mission was successful, but she was deeply relieved when her two-year assignment was over. She longed to return to Palestine and the dangers, deprivations, obstacles, tribulations, inspiration, and work that she had graphically described to her audiences.

Golda was to have her share—more, perhaps, than anyone would ever care to bargain for.

2

2

2

CHAPTER 8

Histadrut

DIRECTLY ON HER return to Palestine in 1934, Golda was invited to join the Executive Committee of Histadrut, and within a year she was elected to the Secretariat, the highest echelon of the "state within a state," and moved on to increasingly difficult and complex assignments. She worked tirelessly at each one and generally achieved the goals she set for herself, but her greatest value to Histadrut was her ability as a troubleshooter who could move into almost any situation as either propagandist, organizer, or fundraiser.

Her success was largely due to her own unshakable conviction of the moral and practical necessity of the programs she espoused or the appeals she made. As a spokesman for Histadrut, she was unmatched for her plain speaking, getting her points over in a style that appealed equally to intellectuals and workers:

"Histadrut is a labor federation unique as a trade union. It had to be. When it was organized in 1920, there were four thousand Jewish workers in the entire country. A big debate was precipitated by a small group who wanted the 'class struggle' to be the main paragraph in the constitution of Histadrut at a time when there was not even a class to struggle against—neither a working class nor a capitalist class. The only struggle that had to be waged was against the swamps and deserts and rocks. And against the settlers' ignorance of physical labor. They were not farmers, they were not masons, they were not road-builders. This was the struggle.

"It required a lot of courage on the part of Ben-Gurion, Berl Katzenelson, and Itzhak Ben-Zvi, who were committed socialists, to realize that the situation in Palestine did not lend itself to dogmatic answers, that we could not with closed eyes passively follow labor movements in other countries and do exactly as they did.

"For us it was not a question of fighting against bad conditions or for more favorable economic conditions. First, something had to be built. So Histadrut became not only an overall trade union but also, since there were no capitalists, its own employer and its own investor."

From this necessity, she explained, Histadrut had achieved or was developing federations of consumers' and producers' cooperatives, marketing, transport, and banking cooperatives, workers' mutual benefit societies, industrial construction companies, and agricultural settlement agencies.

Always she emphasized that Histadrut was not dedicated solely to achieving economic goals but to becoming a moral force in the Yishuv, treasuring, above all, the dignity of the individual not as a tool for something but as the maker of tools.

"Even for the best purposes," she insisted, "it is a crime to turn an individual into simply a means for an ultimate end. A society in which the dignity of the individual is destroyed cannot hope to be a decent society."

She worked almost entirely among men, yet unlike most other women who were making significant contributions toward upbuilding the country, she was not a feminist whose overriding concern was the emancipation of women.

She had always taken feminine equality for granted. "I never found," she said, "that being a woman got in my way. It has been my good fate from an early age to work mainly among men, and it is to their credit that I always felt pretty good about it. I have never expected any privilege from anybody because I am a woman, and the men with whom I worked never treated me less kindly because I was one."

But there was one allowance that the men she worked with had to make for Golda; when she felt she was being criticized unfairly or felt personally offended, she burst into tears. She tried to control this reaction, but she never wholly succeeded.

In 1936 she was made responsible for Histadrut's mutual-aid programs, becoming chairman of the board of directors of Kupat Holim, the Workers' Sick Fund, which provided medical services for nearly one half of the entire Jewish population. Then, as the year ended, she became a member of the Political Department of Histadrut and a representative of the Labor party—Mapai—at sessions of the World Zionist Organization.

In 1937 Golda was again asked to go to the United States, this time to get financial support for a new Histadrut maritime enterprise called Nachson after the legendary biblical figure who was the first to jump into the water when the Israelites crossed the Red Sea. Histadrut planned to build a port at Tel Aviv as a bypass of the Arab-blockaded port at Jaffa and to buy fishing and other vessels, train Jewish seamen, and develop fisheries. The Yishuv in Palestine was enthusiastic about the project, but to convince Americans, who were some six thousand miles away, of the necessity was another matter.

"The sea is an organic economic and political part of Palestine," Golda urged. "And it is yet almost unpossessed. The force which drew us from the city to the farm is now driving us from the land to the sea. We must train our people for work on the seas as we have trained them these many years for work on the soil—one more step toward the independence of our people."

Single-handed, she raised the capital for Project Nachson in a brief and brilliant tour.

What gave more urgency to the building of a port at Tel Aviv was events in Europe which were leading step by step to World War II and which were having devastating repercussions in Palestine.

Between 1933 and 1936 Adolf Hitler's initial persecution of Jews in Germany had impelled some seventy thousand to emigrate to Palestine. Many of these German refugees were professionals—lawyers, doctors, teachers—and others were prosperous businessmen. While the Arabs, led by the mufti, looked with favor on Hitler and his policies, particularly with respect to Jews, and collaborated with him, they were alarmed to see that these policies had boomeranged by bringing to Palestine new resources of Jewish manpower and capital. The Arabs decided that the time had come for pressing their demands on the British Mandate. They had two aims: to compel the Government to abandon the Jewish National Home by halting immigration and restricting land settlement; and by establishing a legislature dominated by Arabs, end up pushing the British out of Palestine.

The Arab push was on—arson, plunder, assassination, and ambush—and it continued right up to the outbreak of World War II in 1939. The British reinforced their troops in Palestine, but the soldiers were largely ineffective against the guerrillas who slipped across the borders at will.

In the kibbutzim and settlements Jews dug trenches and stockaded themselves behind barbed wire, and the Haganah organized road patrols and flying squads which rushed to their aid against Arab marauders. But the Yishuv of some

400,000 people sorely felt the economic pinch of all this disruption, bloodshed, and violence, and emergency measures had to be imposed on the workers to meet the crisis.

Histadrut followed the principle of payment to workers according to need by fixing a basic living wage, to which a supplement was added as the number of the workers' dependents increased. The wage rate for Histadrut officials was computed on the same basis in order that they live like workers and not like officials or bureaucrats. Members also paid their Histadrut dues on a sliding scale, which rose with their salary like an income tax. These dues, used for trade-union and pension funds and health insurance, were paid each month in a lump sum called the single tax. Normally this tax also provided adequately for Histadrut's unemployment fund. But as stores were burned and looted and as factories were sabotaged as a consequence of the Arab riots, the numbers of unemployed rose and the single tax could not meet the situation adequately.

The Histadrut Executive asked its members who were working to agree to an extra tax for a special unemployment fund called Mifdeh, which means ransom or redemption. The idea was that the employed worker had a debt of honor or conscience to pay for his advantage over his comrade who, through no fault of his own, was unemployed. It was a difficult appeal to make, and Golda was designated to try to get the workers to agree and cooperate.

Tempers ran high. The employed workers asked her: "How can I pay more taxes than I already do? Why should I pay for something that's not my fault? This isn't a matter of workers' solidarity, like strike pay. This is something that ought to be the responsibility of the whole community."

And the unemployed workers asked her: "What's the good of being a member of Histadrut if my comrades let my children starve?"

As troubleshooter for Histadrut, Golda cools tempers at a
workers' conference.
(Photo: Alexander Suesskind, Tel Aviv)

Golda faced the angry men out of work and the resentful
men with jobs and cited the facts. Under the Mandate administration, there was no state unemployment insurance
and no funds to which employers and employees were
obliged by law to contribute.

"We live in a community without governmental powers
of coercion and without the possibility of making laws that
are binding on everyone alike," she said. "This community
regards everything that is demanded of it as something
voluntary, and the situation is a bad one, not only for us—
the workers' sector—but for the community as a whole."

And there were some very elementary things, she told the

workers, prosaic and difficult things that were hard to live without. Like clothing. Like food.

"We have among us not only grown-ups who go hungry," she said indignantly, "but also children who are hungry, hungry for bread. We can't go on like this. It is absolutely necessary that one of the first and main things we do will be to wipe out this shame, this blot on the community and chiefly on the Labor Federation."

Many workers countered by suggesting that the Yishuv appeal to Jews of the Diaspora—those Jews who were dispersed all over the world—for help.

But Golda stubbornly opposed seeking relief abroad. "We shall not go to the Jews of the Diaspora to seek relief," she insisted. "Our topics of discussion with them cannot be the matter of unemployment, the matter of hunger, but must center around our efforts to build!"

Eventually, she persuaded the employed workers to pay Mifdeh, not just once, but several times, raising the tax as the number of unemployed continued to rise, at times to about ten thousand. Her personal popularity did not increase with each new appeal she made, but the principle involved was far more important to her than her popularity. She knew that Mifdeh was serving as a precedent and moral example for the whole Yishuv and would make possible the heavy voluntary taxation which the Arab unrest and a looming world war would clearly entail. In the next few years Mifdeh funds would go toward reconstructing ruined settlements, providing for general defense needs, and, of paramount importance, contributing to the huge sums needed for the rescue of European Jews from Nazi concentration camps.

Meanwhile, until the war came, the Arabs continued to riot, to strike, and to press their demands, and a Royal Commission was appointed to examine the Arabs' grievances. It found that the differences between Arabs and Jews could not be reconciled; therefore the Mandate was unworkable, and Palestine would have to be partitioned into Arab and Jewish states with an enclave retained by Britain. The Chamberlain government, after nearly a year's shilly-shally-ing, reversed its original position and called partition "impracticable." Finally, a conference of Arabs and Jews was called in London in 1939. After months of fruitless discussions, during which the Arab delegation refused to deal directly with the Jews, it was called off as a failure.

Shortly thereafter, the formerly pro-Labor and pro-Zionist British Colonial Secretary, Malcolm MacDonald, published the infamous White Paper of 1939. It declared that Jewish immigration to Palestine was limited to a maximum of 75,000 up to March 31, 1944, thereafter suspending it altogether unless the Arabs consented to its continuance. Also, the purchase of land by Jews was virtually prohibited, and within ten years a Palestine state, in which the Jews would always be a minority and live at the sufferance of the Arabs, was to be established.

Although the White Paper was a hands-down victory for the Arabs, they rejected this "solution" as too favorable to the Jews. For their part, the outraged Yishuv charged the Mandate with betrayal of its trust, but foreseeing the desperate need of refugees from the Nazis for a safe haven, had to accept, for the time being, a serious setback to Zionist goals and aspirations.

CHAPTER 9

"Therein Lies Our Strength"

THIS DID NOT mean that the Yishuv was going to cower before the White Paper and offer no resistance to it.

The Jewish National Home in Palestine was not as powerless as it had been. By 1939 the census was 475,000, and the community was full of new enterprise, with a great potential for the further development of its agriculture, industry, and commerce. On the sands of Tel Aviv a city of 100,000 had arisen; Haifa was a booming port; in Jerusalem the Hebrew University, inaugurated in 1925, had greatly expanded; at Rehovot the David Sieff Research Institute, later to become the world-famous Weizmann Institute of Science, was now functioning, and so was the Technion at Haifa. The Workers' Sick Fund of Histadrut, which Golda had headed, and the Hadassah Medical Organization had markedly raised the general health level of the people, and it now compared favorably to that of western countries.

Shortly before the outbreak of World War II, the World Zionist Congress held a meeting in Geneva at which an important difference of opinion developed between two factions over which tactics and strategy would be most effective in the struggle against the White Paper.

Dr. Weizmann's faction believed that the struggle should be confined to political and diplomatic action. "We oppose the use of arms in Palestine except in self-defense," he insisted. "Jews must follow a Jewish course."

But Ben-Gurion was convinced that in addition to political action, the Yishuv must conduct an underground armed struggle against Arab terrorism and the inequities of the White Paper.

"We will fight the White Paper as though there were no war," he declared. "And we will fight the common enemy as though there were no White Paper."

Golda threw her support to Ben-Gurion. To her the issue was once again whether Jews were to stand by helplessly and defenselessly, waiting to be attacked by the Arabs within Palestine and closing their eyes to the plight of fellow Jews under the Nazi terror. She saw no alternative but to fight for a Jewish state and the right of Jews everywhere to emigrate to it, using armed force whenever necessary. In fact, she said, the most powerful secret weapon the Jews had was that there was no alternative.

She was haunted by the hundreds of thousands of Jews who were dying in Hitler's concentration camps, heralding the millions who would meet their deaths in gas chambers and incinerators. It was inconceivable to her that even those fortunate enough to escape should be locked out of Palestine. But the White Paper restricting immigration still stood, and immigration certificates were doled out only to the negligible quotas of refugees who were permitted to enter.

With the outbreak of war, Haapala, or illegal immigration, was the only way entrapped Jews could escape with their lives. Some set out at night from little fishing villages along the Mediterranean coast in leaky vessels, packed to the sinking point and always risking detection by British ships and aircraft and constantly in danger of touching off a mine. After enduring harrowing conditions, including the lack of water and food, the lucky ones landed on a de-

Three orphans of one family who passed through several concentration camps during World War II before they were rescued and brought to Palestine

serted beach along the Palestine coast and were immediately whisked off into the interior and hidden by members of the Haganah, who eagerly waited to receive them. Others reached the coast but were caught by the British and deported to Mauritius, an island in the Indian Ocean off Africa. Still others met the fate of the 202 refugees who drowned in Haifa harbor when the *Patria*, the ship to which they had been transferred for deportation, sank. And many refugees drowned when their unserviceable ships went down at sea or off the rocky Mediterranean shores. In all, over 2,800 Jews perished on their way to Palestine during World War II.

Yet, despite all danger, refugees continued to press toward Palestine and continued to be barred by the British. The British cited as one of their reasons for excluding new immigrants their fear that Axis spies might infiltrate into Palestine and the Middle East if unrestricted immigration were permitted. Also, the British claimed, the enemy had deliberately encouraged the departure of Jews to Palestine in order to "embarrass" Britain by "inflaming Arab sentiments." Appeasement of Mussolini and Hitler had led Britain into war, but she continued to appease the Arabs. Although fighting for her own life in Europe, Britain spared naval vessels to patrol Palestine waters and hunt down the "illegal" ships.

But only if caught were the refugees deported, and no sacrifice was too great for the Yishuv to make certain that the refugees were *not* caught.

Golda wrote in an article for the Women's Labor Council:

> Every day brings forth new edicts, which engulf more hundreds of thousands of people; and we know, we mothers, that there are Jewish children scattered everywhere in the world, and that Jewish mothers in many different countries are asking for only one thing: "Take our children away, take them to any place you choose, only save them from this hell!"
>
> Children have crossed from Germany to Austria, from Austria to Czechoslovakia, and from Czechoslovakia to England—and who can be sure and who can assure their mothers that by getting these children out of one hell, they haven't got them into another?

Even with the situation in the country, with shooting and explosions and political difficulties, the children would be safe only in Palestine.

> Here our children will be safe for the Jewish people. And it's inconceivable that we shan't succeed in our work here, in our toiling to defend every single settlement, even the smallest, if we have before us the picture of thousands of Jews in the various concen-

tration camps. *Therein lies our strength* . . . the
fundamental faith is alive: what they've done to
other peoples and other countries, they won't succeed
in doing to us!

In 1940, when Golda became the head of Histadrut's
Political Department, she was one of those invited by the
Mandate to become a member of the War Economic Advisory Council, established to marshal resources for the war
effort and recruit Jewish soldiers to fight the common
enemy. As a member of the council, Golda negotiated with
the British on behalf of workers engaged in Government
works building roads and camps. But as a member of Haganah, she was also at work helping organize "illegal" immigration of refugees and "illegal" settlement of land.

Despite British prohibitions, a new technique, quasi-
military, was devised for populating isolated and barren
areas of the country. Prefabricated huts, a watchtower, a
stockade, and tents were secretly transported at night to
the chosen site and put into place with the help of dozens of
volunteers, many of them teen-age members of Haganah.
The next morning a new village had been created. Then
these settlements were populated and defended by young
people who adapted better to the rugged terrain and the
threat from Arabs than their elders.

Despite the official ban, at the outbreak of the war
Haganah had about 25,000 men and women and offered a
first draft of 13,000 volunteers to the British military.
Other Jews offered their services individually and served in
all branches. In addition, the British had Haganah intelligence units working behind enemy lines in the Balkans and
Middle East. Repeatedly Jewish volunteers offered to fight
in organized groups similar to the Free Poles or Free
Greeks, but they were rejected until, in 1944, the Churchill
Government permitted the formation of a Jewish Brigade
which fought heroically in the last forty days of the war.

As head of the Political Department of Histadrut, Golda was summoned as a witness at the Sirkin-Richlin trial in 1943, in which two Haganah men were charged with stealing arms from the British military arsenal. Interest in the trial was intense throughout the country, and the challenge confronting Golda was to hold her own against the Government's attempts to worm information about Haganah out of her and yet respond truthfully and responsibly to the cross-questioning.

The prosecutor, a British major, read quotations from various public statements of Golda's which had been filed away for just such a confrontation. But Golda proved unflappable. Not only did she freely admit to what she had said but seized the opportunity to deliver additional messages as to the unity of purpose and morale of the Jewish community.

The major asked Golda whether she was a "nice, peaceful, law-abiding lady." Golda said she thought she was. He followed by reading from a speech she had made on May 2, 1940:

> We, the workers, will combat any appearance of Fascism. The whole Yishuv will join hands in fighting the White Paper. . . . For twenty years we were led to trust the British Government but we have been betrayed. . . . We never taught our youth the use of firearms for offense but for defensive purposes only. . . . And if they are criminals, then all the Jews in Palestine are criminals. . . . MacDonald and his friends are mistaken if they think they can do as they like with us. There are not enough prisons and concentration camps in Palestine to hold all the Jews who are ready to defend their lives and property.

Golda calmly admitted authorship of the statement and added: "Jewish youth will defend Jewish life and property in the event of riots and the necessity to defend life and property. I, as well as other Jews, would defend myself."

The major was not coming off very well in these exchanges. Finally, in another effort to daunt or at least dent her, he read still another passage:

> We must do all in our power to help the illegal immigrants. Britain is trying to prevent the growth and expansion of the Jewish community in Palestine, but it should remember that Jews were here two thousand years before the British came.

All the trial succeeded in accomplishing was to give Golda's statements greater publicity and greater force as her speeches and the postscripts she had added in the courtroom were spread by newspapers, radio, and word of mouth. The Yishuv was intensely proud of "Our Golda."

From 1942 on, Palestine's Jews knew about Hitler's policy of genocide and the extermination camps which were carrying it out. The rest of the world might be incredulous and reject the idea of such monstrous barbarism, but the Yishuv had no such illusions. They knew that millions of Jews were caught in a holocaust—literally being consumed by fire—and felt directly and personally responsible for their fate.

Golda Meyerson provided the Yishuv with a slogan:

"There is no Zionism save the rescue of the Jews!"

Compromise with the Mandate was no longer possible. Because of the White Paper, Zionists must concentrate on securing the withdrawal of the Mandate and the establishment of Palestine as a Jewish state!

Illegal immigration was stepped up, aided by a network of Jewish agents who bribed officials when they could, purchased ships, and established an underground which wrested as many refugees as possible from the Nazi inferno. Haganah fighters blew up British radar stations erected to trap the refugee ships as they reached Palestinian waters and, by still other acts of sabotage, impeded the efforts of the Mandate to carry out the provisions of the White Paper.

By this time the differences between Golda and Moshe Meyerson had proved to be irreconcilable, and they had separated. Menahem, then seventeen, and Sara, fourteen, lived with their mother but also remained affectionately their father's children, too. Golda and the children lived in a workers' cooperative apartment house in Tel Aviv. The four-room apartment was three flights up and afforded a fine, clear view of the sea and beach, making it a most convenient center for observing incoming ships and directing illegal immigration. Normal family life went on also. Menahem, who was already an accomplished cellist, practiced daily in the front room, which became a bedroom at night. Golda slept for those few hours available for sleep on a couch in the living room. Sara and a friend of Golda's shared the bedroom. Except for heavy cleaning chores, which were done by a once-a-week Yemenite maid, Golda kept house and did much of the cooking, ironing, and mending. Especially on Fridays, when all business closed early to observe Shabbat, Golda welcomed the relaxation of making gefilte fish and other traditional foods for her family's meal.

But moments of relaxation were extremely rare, and Golda's doctor ordered her to try to slow up. "She's killing herself!" Menahem complained, but Golda refused to listen and often dragged herself out of a sickbed to go ahead on sheer willpower.

Among her tasks at Haganah headquarters was the writing of leaflets in English, aimed at striking compassion in the hearts of British soldiers who were detailed to seize refugee ships. Unknown to Golda, her daughter Sara, who belonged to the youth group of Haganah, left the apartment at dawn to paste up on walls and billboards the leaflets her mother wrote at night. Even if Golda had been aware of Sara's activity, she would not have questioned her daughter. It was of utmost importance for all Haganah activities, at whatever level, to be kept as secret as possible, for only in this way lay safety for both the individuals and the units involved. Meanwhile, teen-agers like Menahem and Sara were acquiring valuable practice in tactics that would shape the Haganah into an extremely effective fighting force when the time came for a showdown.

Another of Golda's Haganah tasks was to write material to be broadcast by a secret radio, which called itself the Voice of Israel. The broadcasts kept the Yishuv informed about the state of affairs, despite British censorship, and presented the Jewish side of the struggle to the Arabs and British soldiers. Broadcasts were made from various apartments in Tel Aviv and shifted from day to day. Golda had to compose texts at the last moment, on the morning of the broadcast.

At last World War II ended in 1945, and most of the Jewish survivors of the holocaust had no place to go except Palestine. Yet the Labour Government which came into power that year decided to maintain the White Paper in force despite all its previous pledges to rescind it.

Golda appealed to "our friends and comrades in the British Labour Government" with a cry from the heart, which she hoped would sting them into an awareness of the deep injustice they were inflicting and at the same time warn them that the Yishuv would not lie down and take it:

". . . Many of us have already met people who've come from 'there'—from the brink of death. It's hard for us—we don't want to fight you. We want to build, to construct. We want the remnants of our people, those few who remain, to come here in peace, to build and construct and create alongside us. But if not, then you must understand in the clearest possible manner: we have no choice.

"Of our people no more than two-thirds remain. That number we will not reduce of our own free will, unless it be when we fall in the fight against injustice, against the wrong you are going to inflict on us. But we will not aid and abet you of our free will by keeping the peace; we will not help you reduce the small number of rescued Jewish children by even one single child."

She was not asking for pity or charity or mercy because none had been shown all during the years of mass murder when the British Government in Palestine had not lifted a finger to save even one Jewish refugee.

She did not ask, but demanded: "The right of a people that wants to live, the right of a people that has felt what it is to lose millions of its sons, *this right:* to come to its own country, to settle, to build, to live here as a free people in its own independent state, with all friendliness and loyalty to its neighbors, to other countries, to all the peoples of the world—that's what we demand!"

CHAPTER 10

Survivors of the Holocaust

THE JEWS WHO had survived the holocaust were liberated from concentration camps only to be held in D.P. (displaced persons) camps in Germany and Austria. Responding to the urgings of American Jewry and his own deeply humanitarian feelings, President Harry S Truman put pressure on the British to agree to the appointment of an Anglo-American Commission of Enquiry consisting of six Americans and six Britons who, after visiting the D.P. camps and Palestine, were to recommend what must be done to help the refugees.

In Jerusalem on March 25, 1946, Golda Meyerson appeared before the commission to testify on behalf of Histadrut:

"I do not know, gentlemen, whether you who are fortunate enough to belong to the two great democratic nations of Britain and America can realize—with the best will and intention to understand our problems—what it means to belong to a people which is constantly questioned about its very existence. . . . We are constantly being questioned as to whether we have a right to be Jews. We are not better, but not worse, than others, with our own language, our own culture, the right just as others to determine our own lives, to live in friendship and cooperation with those near and far. . . .

"The mass of Jewish workers in this country has decided

Youth from Germany arrive in the Tel Aviv harbor and celebrate their rescue with a dance.

to end during our lifetime this helplessness, this lack of security, this dependence upon others. All we desire is that which all peoples in this world have as their natural right —the right to be masters of our own fate, and our fate alone, not that of others. . . . We want the possibility of bringing up large numbers of Jewish children, born here, free of fear, with their heads high."

As usual, Golda spoke extemporaneously, looking at each member of the commission in turn, reaching out toward them, and it was apparent that they were moved. When she had finished, one of the American members asked: "Where did you learn to speak such fluent English, Mrs. Meyerson?"

Golda smiled. "I'm from Milwaukee, so it's not strange at all."

In April, 1946, the commission unanimously recommended the immediate admission of 100,000 refugees into Palestine and the abrogation of the White Paper restrictions on land sales to Jews. But the British Government reneged on its original promise to be bound by any unanimous proposals of the commission. Instead, proposals and counterproposals were made which were unacceptable either to the Arabs or to the Jews.

Then, in October, 1946, President Truman publicly declared his support of the proposal of the Jewish Agency for "a viable Jewish state in control of its own immigration and economic policies in an adequate area of Palestine instead of the whole of Palestine." Also, he insisted that sizable immigration of refugees to Palestine should begin at once and not wait for a solution of the whole Palestine problem.

But Britain disagreed and continued to place roadblocks in the path of any just and humane settlement.

Tension and fighting in Palestine erupted again.

A typical occurrence under the British Mandate was reported by international news services:

"FOUR FREEDOMS" REFUGEES BATTLE BRITISH CREW
FOR RIGHT TO LAND IN PALESTINE

One thousand visa-less Jewish refugees desperately determined to land in Palestine, battled fiercely against sailors of the Royal Navy who boarded their 400-ton blockade runner the *Four Freedoms* off the Palestine coast in an attempt to divert her from Tel Aviv to the port of Haifa where deportation ships wait to take the refugees to Cyprus.

A number of British sailors were injured in the fight, but they finally managed to secure a line from the destroyer *Childers* which towed the refugee ship to Haifa. Twelve of the refugees were seen jumping overboard, apparently in a do-or-die attempt to reach Palestine's shores.

One of those who dived overboard was a twenty-year-old man who swam for nine hours, eluding naval craft and police launches. He came ashore safely and was hidden by the Haganah in a Jewish settlement, but a companion who took the plunge with him vanished and was believed to have drowned.

The young survivor made an anonymous statement to the press which should have convinced the British that they were fighting not only an ignominious but a losing battle. "Like myself," the young man said, "thousands of others will escape the British blockade net and will arrive in our homeland. As long as I live, I will never forget or forgive this encounter with Britain."

Two weeks later the Haganah retaliated for the capture of the refugee ship with a unit of frogmen who laid explosive charges which seriously damaged one of the British deportation ships lying at anchor in Haifa Bay.

Not all the Jewish reprisals against the British blockade were violent; some protests, as in the famous instance of the refugee ship *Feda,* relied on moral persuasion and succeeded.

In their war against illegal immigration the British began to send warships to the ports of embarkation of vessels seeking to run the blockade. In the Italian port of La Spezia, hundreds of refugees aboard the *Feda* went on a hunger strike in protest against being prevented from sailing. Golda Meyerson proposed to the heads of the Jewish community that they join the hunger strike on the *Feda* and keep it going, to the death if necessary, until the refugees were permitted to enter Palestine. Three days before Passover of 1946, Golda and the others began their fast.

In Kiev forty-three years before, little Golda Mabovitz had insisted on joining the adults in their synagogue fast against the Kishinev pogrom, and she had stuck to her guns. That fast lasted a single day. This one lasted over four days—101 hours—until the British High Commissioner promised to release the *Feda* and permit the entry of all its passengers. Golda was hospitalized for a few days after the fast was over, but that mattered not at all. The tactic had been successful!

The British continued to step up their efforts to break the back of Jewish resistance and raided villages suspected of hiding arms or of offering a haven to illegal immigrants. Frustrated in these attempts, they decided on the most drastic action to date. On June 29, 1946, British soldiers raided Jewish Agency headquarters in Jerusalem arresting and interning its leaders in a prison camp at Latrun. David Ben-Gurion, head of the agency, escaped arrest only because he happened to be in Paris.

When the soldiers came to seize Golda, she stood her ground. "You cannot do it!" she said imperiously. Reaching for the telephone, she called the United States Consulate and others to tell them what was happening, and the bewildered soldiers went away without her.

On that day, known throughout the country as Black Sabbath, 2,178 men and women were taken into custody, and a full-scale British military operation was launched to liquidate the Haganah. But Haganah intelligence learned of the plan and countered by evading the British and blowing up the bridges over the Jordan River.

The head of the Jewish Agency's Political Department, Moshe Sharett, had been arrested, and Golda was called upon to replace him. In doing so, she was really taking over the shadow Foreign Office of a shadow Jewish Government. It was an extremely exposed and delicate position, and she did not feel that she had the background or training for it, but she consented, hoping that she would be relieved as soon as Sharett was released from prison camp. Gradually, the British freed the agency leaders, but it was decided that Sharett should head the Political Department of the Jewish Agency from Washington. Instead of a brief tenure, Golda was compelled to remain at her Jerusalem post all through the stormy year of 1947.

Within a couple of months of Golda's take-over as head of the department, a particularly brutal raid was made on two settlements in the Negev, the desert area which only the most courageous and hardy Jewish pioneers were attempting to settle and reclaim. The tiny settlement at Ruhama, on the fringe of the Negev, had been destroyed twice in the past by Arab marauders only to be rebuilt by the Jewish settlers. Now British troops went on a rampage and using scrapers and bulldozers, razed or damaged every dwelling and farm building. The floor of the communal dining room was ripped up, and a trench the length of the building dug in the earth in a search for arms caches. Soldiers bashed in the radiator of the settlement's only tractor and crippled its water supply. When the settlers protested, the officer in charge replied that they must reveal their arms, or everything in the settlement would be ploughed under or burned.

Golda now represented the Yishuv in all discussions with the Mandate authorities. Her response to this outrage was, as usual, immediate and uncompromising.

Acts like these in the Negev, she said, could not bring about the pacification of the country or ease the tensions. The Negev settlements had never denied the possession of arms for defensive purposes. The settlers claimed that it would have been impossible under present conditions to survive in that part of the country without arms. To take away the settlement's arms was an open invitation to destruction.

"As long as there is no convincing guarantee that effective defense for these settlements will be forthcoming from the other side," Golda insisted, "the Jews cannot forgo their arms."

Not once did Golda refer to her own personal involvement with Negev settlements. But in 1943 her seventeen-year-old daughter, Sara, had volunteered to join a group of young pioneers to establish a kibbutz called Revivim, in the southernmost and most isolated of the Jewish settlements in the desert. Sara was picking up at Revivim where her mother had left off at Merhavia, and while Golda was immensely proud of Sara's courage and resolution, she was also deeply concerned for her daughter's safety. In the long run, though, Golda felt that a Jew was safer even in a kibbutz in the Negev than anywhere else in the world.

Her son, Menahem, who was living with her in Tel Aviv, was pursuing a far different course from his sister's. He was already a cellist with the Palestine Symphony Orchestra and had decided to devote himself to music.

When Menahem and Sara were young children, they were often hurt and angry over what they felt was their mother's neglect of them, and Golda admitted that there were conflicts. In the long run, though, Golda felt that her activities enriched their lives by broadening the narrow horizon and limits of the family.

A reporter had asked Sara whether she felt neglected as

a child. "Yes," Sara said, "but for such a mother, it was worthwhile."

Although the Mandate authorities knew that Golda worked closely with their adversaries, the Haganah leaders, they respected her personal integrity and staunch defense of her people. More militant Jews had formed groups like the Irgun Zvai Leumi and the Stern gang and had embarked on a program of terrorist activities which were appalling to much of the Yishuv, but when Golda was asked by the British to cooperate in tracking them down, she would not budge from her position.

"We cannot become a nation of informers," she said flatly. "We cannot make informers of six hundred thousand Jews, each one watching his neighbor or friend."

Among the more heartbreaking situations, with respect to refugees, were the children in the internment camps on Cyprus, so near and yet so very far from the haven Palestine offered. By November, 1947, the camps were so overcrowded and the living conditions so harsh that in many ways the refugees were worse off than they had been in the D.P. camps. While some seven thousand "captured" refugees had been admitted to Palestine on the legal monthly immigration quota, the latest arrivals would have a two-year wait.

Jewish doctors, kindergarten teachers, and social workers in Palestine went as volunteers to serve the Cyprus refugees. They reported that they were afraid of what would happen over the winter to the babies a year old or less. The Jewish Agency negotiated with the British for the early release of families with babies and obtained their consent to give them priority on the immigration quota. But how to persuade the refugees themselves to give up their precious quota number to families with children? To do so was such a profoundly difficult and distasteful task that only Golda volunteered to undertake it.

What followed then was one of the most moving experiences of her life, and she was never able to describe it without blinking back the tears.

"I saw people in the Cyprus camps, and I can't tell you what conditions were like there. These people came from camps in Germany behind barbed wire to camps in Cyprus behind barbed wire. There was not a blade of grass, just miserable tents, yet some of our people had gone to live there and help out. I wondered at them. How can they live there? How can they manage it? How can they do what they are doing?

"There were children in Cyprus who had never seen a live flower. They had never held a rose or any other flower in their hands. But our volunteer kindergarten teachers had taught them to make flowers out of paper, and when I arrived on the island, a child gave me a whole bouquet of paper flowers. No bouquet I have ever received or ever shall receive will be more beautiful than the paper flowers from the children of Cyprus."

Golda slogged through the mud of the camp and talked to bachelors and single girls and to married couples without children and pleaded with them to help save the lives of the babies of Cyprus by giving up their own places on the quota. Somehow she got through to them how urgent their sacrifice was and won their consent. Ten days later the British freighter *Ocean Vigour* steamed into Haifa from Cyprus with 1,420 persons, the first contingent of infants with their parents. Another group of 2,400, including 2,100 orphan youths under eighteen and 100 infants under two years of age, arrived shortly after, aboard a vessel chartered by the Jewish Agency.

But Golda had witnessed the misery of the prisoners on Cyprus, who already had concentration-camp numbers branded on their arms, and she was filled with misgivings about the future.

"Can these people who have gone through hell, can they

really live again?" she wondered. "Can they live for themselves even, let alone do something for the country or for somebody else?"

Years later Golda received her answer. "Oh," she sighed, "there are some lovely moments that make up for a lot. I was visiting a kibbutz in the Negev and a woman came up to me. 'At last I have a chance to thank you,' she said. 'I was on Cyprus and I had a baby girl. Where would she be without what you did?' What a wonderful feeling! This baby girl is now finishing her army service and Israel is that much stronger because of her.

"Somebody said," she added, laughing, "that the Jewish people is a crazy people. They get crazy ideas and they implement them. I don't know whether we are crazy; maybe it's ultrasanity we had to be able to prepare these people who were broken in spirit and body, these children who had lost faith in everything and in everybody, to grow up devoted to ideals, prepared to give their lives for these ideals, to believe in the future of our people and in the future of the world."

That first contingent of refugees from Cyprus arrived in Palestine in time to celebrate the greatest day of rejoicing ever known by the Yishuv. On November 29, 1947, the General Assembly of the United Nations passed a resolution for the partition of Palestine into an independent Jewish state, an independent Arab state, and an internationalized Jerusalem.

There was dancing in the streets that day, but the rejoicing was short-lived. The next day, the Arabs, who had rejected the United Nations partition, mounted riots and acts of terror against the Jewish state which was not yet born.

CHAPTER 11

The Will to Resist

A DAY AFTER partition, on November 30, 1947, Golda Meyerson addressed a huge public gathering in Jerusalem and appealed directly to the Arabs: "Our hand is offered to you in peace and friendship. Take the proffered hand!"

A few hours later the first Jewish victims of Arab attacks were being buried. Between November 30 and December 31, 1947, skirmishes between Jews and Arabs had resulted in 1,345 casualties: 203 Arabs and 193 Jews killed; 14 British soldiers, 5 British police, and 6 civilians of assorted nationalities also killed; and the remainder injured.

On December 26, the Jerusalem papers reported that 7 Jews were killed and 8 wounded in an Arab attack on two Jewish convoys, "one of which was carrying Golda Meyerson, head of the Jewish Agency's Political Department in Jerusalem." The ambush had taken place near an Arab village a short distance from Jerusalem, even though the Mandate authorities had given assurances that the Jerusalem-Jaffa highway was heavily protected and safe. The passengers in the convoy reported that in the entire forty-mile trip they had encountered only two British armored police cars. This was extremely scanty protection for which there was no excuse. The Mandate Government had been instructed to leave "at the earliest possible date," but until they did so, they were supposed to be responsible for the people's safety.

Golda speaking to young settlers who are determined to remain on their land even at the cost of their lives

Naturally, in her official capacity Golda protested to the Mandate authorities over their laxness. Since the partition, she had been meeting with them almost daily going over much the same territory and accomplishing very little.

"I take up the problem of safety of the roads to Tel Aviv," she explained to reporters. "When I ask why the Government is not patrolling the road more effectively, I am promised that things are now in hand and absolutely safe. Then it just so happens—I really do not do it on purpose—that I go down to Tel Aviv the next day and my convoy is involved in a very serious attack. People in the convoy are killed and wounded. And when I go back to the Government and repeat the same question, I get the same promises over and over again. . . ."

Again, on December 31, 1947, less than a week after her convoy had been ambushed, Golda and other Jewish Agency officials were traveling from Jerusalem to Tel Aviv to meet Moshe Sharett, who had just returned from the United States. The official party, traveling in a convoy of Jewish Agency cars and public buses, had detoured to avoid the Arab town of Er Ramle but ran into a British police roadblock. Their cars were searched for weapons, and when a young Haganah girl, assigned to Golda as a bodyguard, was found to possess a gun, the British tried to arrest her.

"If you arrest her, you arrest me, too," Golda warned the police. "If anyone is to blame for the arms, it is I."

They decided to hold the girl overnight, and Golda stayed with her, effecting her release next morning when both of them proceeded to the meeting in Tel Aviv.

"Yes," Golda commented to reporters, "we are usually promised that we shall not be searched for arms if they are not used to attack. But the next day it happens that I myself go down to Tel Aviv, and my convoy is stopped and searched for arms."

She did not add that more than once she had hidden purloined British Sten guns under her skirts and transported them for the Haganah.

Despite her tremendous responsibilities and the peril to her own life in carrying them through, Golda always managed to take time out for her family and friends and to give selflessly of herself when needed.

While her sister Shana was in New York undergoing surgery, Shana's son, Yona, in the urgency of the times, decided to marry a girl he had met in the Haganah without waiting for his mother's return. Aunt Golda stepped into the breach. She baked all the cakes for the wedding and made all the arrangements which entailed trips from Tel Aviv to Shana's house in Holon over a road that was constantly under Arab sniper fire. But how important was that? Her nephew was getting married!

Joyful respites like weddings were very few indeed. As the year 1947 drew to a close, Golda volunteered to go on a fund-raising mission to the United States. Money was urgently needed for arms, particularly since the Yishuv knew that once statehood was declared, it would be all-out war with the Arabs, not merely skirmishing. Moreover, on December 5, the United States had suddenly clapped an embargo on the sale of all arms to the Middle East. Arabs were also included in this embargo, but they were already well equipped. They had reportedly bought more than $37 million worth of American arms left over from World War II, and they had large stores of additional arms from the British who would continue to supply them. Estimates placed Arab strength at fifty thousand mobilized troops, not including reserves, with artillery, armor, and an air force.

Afraid that the United Nations would not approve of the partition if it knew how poorly equipped they were to defend themselves, the Jews had bluffed so well about the strength of their forces that the Arabs were fooled, and the United Nations' own estimate was extremely unrealistic. In reality the Palmach, which was the Haganah's only fully trained and organized striking force, numbered only three thousand, a few hundred of them girls. On the day of partition the Haganah had only ten thousand rifles, nineteen hundred Sten guns, and sixty-six mortars. It had no heavy armaments, no artillery, no armored cars, nothing to put into the skies or on the seas.

Golda arrived in New York in mid-January, 1948. Advance reports were that it was hopeless to expect American Jewry, whose funds were depleted by years of contributions to Hitler's victims, to raise more than $5 to $7 million. Two days after her arrival a conference of the Council of Jewish Federations was to take place in Chicago, but several of Golda's advisers cautioned her against appealing to this group, since it was not a Zionist convention and the conference agenda was packed.

Her younger sister, Mrs. Clara Stern, who was a coordinator for the council, urged her to go.

"The smartest thing you can do," Clara said, "is take the next plane to Chicago and crack the ice there."

Golda took her advice and managed to get herself squeezed onto the agenda. She described her mission in typically forthright terms: "I came for this very simple thing: to get in cash, in two or three weeks, twenty-five million dollars. Very simple. Since I have no idea what twenty-five million dollars really means, what it looks like, I know from nothing: I need twenty-five million dollars in a few weeks."

As usual, she spoke without notes, and she needed none. The story of Palestine's struggle was her own story. Its life was the life she had led at the forefront of the Yishuv for over twenty years. She spoke from the heart, but she also piled up the facts, and the facts carried their own weight of truth, moving even the hardheaded, powerful men of finance and industry who were in her audience.

"Every Jew in the country knows that within a few months a Jewish state in Palestine will be established," she said. "We have to pay for it. We know that the price we have to pay will be the lives of the best of our people. A little over three hundred have already been killed. There will be more. There is no doubt that there will be more. But there is no doubt that the spirit of our young people will not falter. The spirit is there. But this spirit alone cannot face rifles and machine guns. Rifles and machine guns without spirit are not worth very much, but spirit without these in time can be broken with the body. . . .

"You cannot decide whether we will fight or not. We will. No white flag of the Jewish community will be raised for the mufti. The decision is taken. Nobody can change that. You can change only one thing—whether we shall be victorious. Yes, whether we fight or not, this is a decision *we* have to make. Whether we live or not, this is a decision *you* have to make.

"Is it possible," she asked, "that the youngsters who are in the front lines will have to fall because the money that should have reached Palestine today will reach it in two months?"

The $25 million she asked for was forthcoming at once from community leaders who pledged the sum and then set about arranging for bank loans to make the cash available immediately.

Rarely using planes or even Pullman trains in an effort to save expenses, Golda traveled all over the country, frequently by bus. She was anxious to reach not only the wealthy Jews of America but also the working-class communities as well. This was the class she had sprung from, and she had never lost touch with them. Once, out West, an official welcoming delegation of workers missed her arrival at the bus terminal. In tears the head of the delegation phoned her hotel. Golda understood. She repacked her valise, walked back to the bus terminal, and the greeting ceremony took place as scheduled.

Golda said to them: "If we have something to fight with, we'll fight with that. If we don't, we'll fight with stones if necessary."

The workers understood and reached for their savings-account books.

She returned to Palestine, having raised fifty million dollars in two and a half months. She told friends that she could now regard herself as a great "schnorrer," which is Yiddish for "beggar."

But David Ben-Gurion was more gallant. "Someday when

history will be written," he observed, "it will be said that there was a Jewish woman who got the money which made the state [of Israel] possible."

Now, with the millions Golda had raised, one of the most fantastic, secret arms-purchasing-and-supply schemes ever recorded slipped into high gear. It had been set in motion in 1945 by Ben-Gurion during a visit to New York. Under the supervision and coordination of Haganah teams sent from Palestine, a countrywide network of American business executives, engineers, scientists, and students had been woven. Their task was to acquire and transship despite the United States arms embargo, the guns, planes, and armored equipment—the military arsenal, in short—that the not-yet-born state of Israel must have to defend itself.

An American college student transported loads of contraband gunpowder in a Cadillac, the only car that would not reveal the weight it was carrying. A group of electronics "whiz kids" from a New York high school put together the necessary parts for a secret radio network to link the isolated Jewish settlements and warn them of Arab raiding parties. An American lawyer who had been a member of the Office of Strategic Services—America's cloak-and-dagger World War II unit—organized and ran a secret school in the heart of New York City to train young Palestinians for intelligence work, familiarizing them with the use of codes and ciphers and with espionage and commando tactics. "Graduates" of this school returned to Palestine and became known as the Shoo-Shoo boys, Hebrew slang for secret agents. Other members of this underground designed guns, bought surplus supplies, such as a Constellation airplane for $15,000 ($750 down) and a baby flattop, the Attu, for $125,000, and managed to ship out these illegal cargoes under dozens of ingenious disguises and improvisations.

At a press conference in New York just prior to leaving on her fund-raising tour, Golda justified the Yishuv's resort to "illegal" arms:

"We know that we are breaking the law when we use illegal arms," she said. "But if Jews are to be good, law-abiding citizens, then we must sit back and wait for the Arabs to decide whether they will snipe and kill or not kill. If we are killed, at least we are killed as law-abiding citizens. Well," she concluded, "with the choice between being killed as law-abiding citizens or living as lawbreakers, we choose the second alternative and we break the law by using illegal arms."

When Golda returned to Palestine in March, 1948, she learned that the Haganah had been compelled to abandon attempts to supply the Negev settlements by land. The narrow, curving inland road had proved too vulnerable to ambush by the Arabs, and the coastal road, which ran through densely populated Arab towns and villages, was too heavily mined. Only two Piper Cubs could now maintain contact with the isolated settlements in the southern desert—among them, her daughter Sara's kibbutz at Revivim.

Then, on April 14, 1948, the whole Yishuv was wracked by the Arab ambush and massacre of a convoy which had set out to evacuate hospital equipment and supplies from the Hadassah Hospital on Mount Scopus. While going through the Arab Quarter, the head of the hospital, Dr. Haim Yassky, and seventy-five of Israel's outstanding physicians, scientists, and nurses were murdered in a daylong attack. The British soldiers, only a few yards from the scene, stood by and did nothing.

Despite all the purchasing and scrounging, six weeks before the end of the Mandate, scheduled for May 14, the Yishuv still had no fighter planes, no tanks, no artillery, and insufficient small arms. Ben-Gurion called a council of war attended by Golda Meyerson, Jacob Dostrovsky, chief of staff of the Haganah, and Yigael Yadin, a scholarly archaeologist who had joined the Haganah at the age of fifteen and who was now its director of operations. They decided to dispatch one of their most experienced secret agents to Europe in search of planes.

With irony, which was certainly not lost on the Jews, the agent succeeded in purchasing surplus German Messerschmitt fighter planes from the Czechs, who had been taken over by the Communists in February, 1948. The Czechs cooperated enthusiastically: They gave the pilots, most of whom were American Jewish volunteers, instruction in flying the German planes and as a masterly finishing touch, provided them with coveralls left behind by the Germans which had swastikas sewed on their backs.

Much of this time, Golda Meyerson was in Jerusalem with the authority, in the event that it became impossible to contact Ben-Gurion in Tel Aviv, to deal with all defense matters in the city and the surrounding area, including reacting to Arab attacks and the prevention of any onslaught against any part of the city. In addition to this semimilitary role, Golda had another sideline, smuggling weapons.

When she could not reach Ben-Gurion by wireless or by road to Tel Aviv, Golda boarded a "primus," a tiny plane, and flew to the north shore of the Dead Sea. There she transferred to a British-protected convoy of trucks loaded with phosphates for transport to Tel Aviv. What the British did not know was that the "primus" that carried Golda also carried caches of weapons.

"On a number of occasions I sat next to the driver of one of the trucks knowing that besides the sacks of phosphates were sacks of weapons which had been unloaded under the very noses of the British!" Golda laughed. "Unfortunately, the critical shortage of arms in Tel Aviv did not permit the sending of any large amount to Jerusalem whose situation was much more critical. We lacked not only guns but food as well. Jerusalem had very little of anything"— except, as everywhere else in the Yishuv, the will to resist.

CHAPTER 12

"They Shall No More Be Plucked Out of Their Land"

THE ONLY ARAB neighbor who offered even a remote possibility of remaining neutral in the war, which would inevitably ensue after the Mandate Government withdrew from Palestine, was Trans-Jordan, under the leadership of King Abdullah ibn-Hussein. Abdullah had been installed in 1921 as emir, when Winston Churchill, then British Colonial Secretary, amputated Trans-Jordan from Palestine as another of the Empire's efforts to appease the Arabs. Abdullah became king in 1946 when the country gained its independence. Abdullah had been friendly toward the Jews, not because he loved them so much but because he hated and feared their mutual enemy, the mufti of Jerusalem, more.

Shortly before partition, in November, 1947, Abdullah, in a secret meeting with Golda at the home of the director of the electric power station near Naharayia, had let it be known that he was interested in exploring the possibility of preventing an Arab-Jewish war. Such a war would go against his own interests, since any Arab state created in Palestine would be headed by the mufti, and Golda's task was to persuade Abdullah that, therefore, he should not join in the invasion plans of the Arab League.

"He promised, in a rather elegant fashion, that he would never join the forces which were preparing to attack us," Golda reported to her colleagues. "He had always been a

103

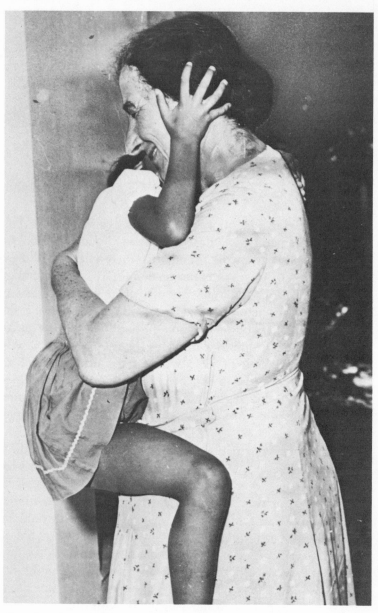

Grandmother Golda hugs her grandchild, a second-generation sabra.

friend. We had the same common enemy: the mufti. Abdullah wanted to live in peace with us. He told me that after the United Nations reached its decision [on partition] we would meet again to discuss how we would live together in the future."

What Abdullah hoped to accomplish after the partition was to annex the Arab portion of Palestine. "I want to add this portion to my kingdom," he told Golda. "I do not want a new Arab state, which would interfere with my plans and enable the other Arabs to boss me."

After partition, conditions in the country were too disturbed to hold another meeting with Abdullah, but Golda began to hear rumors that despite his promise, his Arab Legion would go to war against the Jews along with the other members of the Arab League. Abdullah had taken his doctor into his confidence, and he acted as an intermediary, bringing Golda various messages from the king and, in turn, delivering her replies which at times took the form of questions, listing things that were disturbing to the Jewish community. Why, she now asked, despite his assurances that he would not attack, did rumors to the contrary continue to reach her? The question seemed artless enough, but tucked in the back of Golda's mind was Abdullah's having asked her what the attitude of the Jews would be to a proposal to include a Jewish state in his kingdom. Was that the way the wind was now blowing?

The doctor brought Golda an interesting reply. Abdullah expressed surprise that she had posed such a question and wanted her to know three things: (1) He was a king, and a king always kept his promises; (2) he was a Bedouin, and a Bedouin never went back on his word; and (3) a king would never retract a promise made to a woman. Therefore, the doctor said, Golda must remain confident that nothing untoward was going to happen.

The rumors continued, however, and Golda asked the head

of the electrical works at Naharayia to try to arrange another meeting for her with Abdullah.

Golda returned to Jerusalem, expecting to remain there, but she had no sooner reached the city than a reply came from Abdullah that he was willing to meet her. He laid down the condition, though, that Golda come to him in Amman, Trans-Jordan's capital, since it was now too dangerous for him to go to Naharayia. For Golda to go to Amman would also be risky: The Jordanian army was massing and coming toward Jewish territory, and to reach the capital meant going three hundred miles in the opposite direction, right into the arms of the enemy. As a postscript to his invitation, King Abdullah added that it would be most unwise to inform his troops that he was expecting a Jewish guest, and since he could not guarantee safe conduct, Golda would have to make the trip on her own responsibility.

Golda did not hesitate. To reach Amman, she must return to Tel Aviv, which, on May 9, only five days before the Mandate ended, was not a particularly safe journey. She was asked to be at the improvised airstrip in Jerusalem at ten o'clock in the morning ready for takeoff, but the plane from Tel Aviv did not arrive till seven o'clock that night. It was a small plane with an open cockpit. Shortly after a difficult takeoff the pilot received a radio message from Tel Aviv warning him not to make the flight because of the strong winds. But by that time they were well on their way to the Sde Dov airfield at Tel Aviv, and they completed the flight.

Next day Golda left for Haifa, where a seamstress whipped up an Arab dress, complete with veils and shawls, as a disguise. There she was joined by her escort and interpreter, Ezra Danin, an Oriental Jew whose grandmother had been born in Baghdad. Danin had been chosen for the mission because he was fluent in both Arabic and Hebrew. He knew Golda well, having worked with her for many years in the "sweet-and-bitter times," when he was a member of the Zionist Executive. During the Mandate he was involved with security as an intelligence officer of the Haganah on Arab affairs.

Danin learned of the proposed meeting with Abdullah while attending a berith, or circumcision, at which he was acting as godfather. He had to leave the party at once and meet Golda in Haifa.

"It's useless to go," Danin told her.

Golda asked, "Are you frightened?"

"No."

"Why not?" she demanded.

"I've faced death a hundred times," Danin replied. "This is another time. But why should you, a woman, go? Not only are you a woman but you don't know Arabic, and you're going right into Arab country while they're mobilizing their troops. You shouldn't have to go."

Golda shook her head. "If there's the slightest chance of saving the life of even one young man, I'll go."

That night, one of the king's aides, a Bedouin whom the king had raised and educated, called for Golda and Danin to drive them to his home, where the meeting would take place. Along the way, the car was stopped a dozen times at various checkpoints. The driver and Danin aroused no suspicion, and Golda, swathed in her veils and shawls, sitting very quietly in the back seat, did not draw special attention to herself.

Soon after their arrival at the aide's splendid house, King Abdullah left his palace and joined them.

Golda requested that the king keep his promise, reminding him of the three points he had made to the doctor.

The king did not deny that he had made the promise.

"It is true that I promised," he said, "for at that time I thought that I was master over my own acts and that I would be able to fulfill an undertaking which I regarded as just. Since then, I have discovered that I am not the master I thought I was."

Neither Golda nor Danin needed to hear much else, for

the king's meaning was clear: He would be going to war against them.

The king, though, continued talking, indicating that there was a way of preventing war. "I don't know why you are so impatient," he said. "Don't establish a Jewish state now. Agree to delay the matter of immigration of Jews. I shall take over the country and you can be represented in Parliament and I can assure you of good relations. By doing this you can prevent war."

Impatient? Golda thought. The Jews had been patient for more than two thousand years! She realized that she did not have the authority to accept or reject the king's proposal, but she told him that she saw no point in even bringing the matter before her colleagues. She could give him the answer on the spot.

"You have always been a friend of ours and have followed our fortunes with close interest," she said. "Do you believe that we have done all we have simply to be represented in someone else's Parliament? You know our aspirations and what we hope to obtain. If the only alternative which you offer is war, then let it be war. Naturally, I hope we will win. We will meet afterward."

As he prepared to leave, the king turned to Danin. "You didn't help me," he said, meaning that as one born in the East, Danin ought to have helped him influence Golda to change her mind.

Golda and Danin were then invited by their host to a sumptuous Oriental meal, at which she was given the guest of honor's chair. It was after midnight, and Danin was starved. But Golda, too tense to eat, helped herself to a small piece of mutton, nibbled at it briefly, and ate nothing else.

When they prepared to enter the car for the return journey, Golda turned to Danin.

"What will happen now, Ezra?" she asked.

Danin was very grumpy. "If we win, we'll have ten thousand casualties," he snapped. "If we lose, we'll have fifty thousand."

Golda frowned. "You're a very hard man. Why are you angry? What did I do to you?"

"I tell you, Golda, I'm hungry."

"Well, who compelled you not to eat?"

Ezra grinned. "You did."

Then he told her that according to Arab etiquette, when the guest of honor at a meal stopped eating, so must everyone else. If she had not felt like eating, she should have continued nibbling at something while the others ate their fill. She had finished her bite of mutton and then been too preoccupied to notice that the others had also stopped eating.

Golda shrugged, but fifteen years later when she was Foreign Minister, she told a party of three hundred people what had happened at Abdullah's feast and publicly apologized to Ezra for keeping him hungry.

By the time they headed back to Naharayia, there was virtually a state of war, and Jordanian troops were already closing in on the town. Their Arab driver dropped them at a bridge over a dry riverbed. They would have to walk along this stretch of no-man's-land for a distance of two to three miles before they reached the Haganah guard who was waiting to lead them to safety.

"Are you frightened?" Danin asked Golda.

"Are you?"

Danin shook his head. "I told you I'm a fatalist. I have no feeling at all now."

"Well," Golda said, her voice shaking ever so slightly, "I don't feel at all like a heroine, but I did have to do my duty."

Fortunately, the banks of the riverbed hid them from view, for had they been sighted by a Jordanian patrol, they would have been shot on sight. The blessed young

Haganah soldier awaited them as planned, and the long, black night was over.

Directly from her meeting with King Abdullah, Golda went to Tel Aviv to a meeting of the leadership of the Mapai party. Only two or three members present knew where Golda had been, and, of course, they wanted to know whether there was any hope. Sadly, Golda told them she had no good news, but that it was her impression that Abdullah was going to war reluctantly, having been drawn into a net laid for him by the other Arab states and the machinations of the British.

Bad news or not, decisions about the proclamation of the new state must be made and all arrangements finalized. Haganah leaders were called in and asked their opinion as to what the chances were of withstanding the full-scale invasion by the Arabs when the British withdrew. The Haganah leaders replied that they could not offer better than even odds.

"So we're going to be attacked by six Arab countries and we have fourteen thousand rifles," Golda said. "That's what we are going to war with, but we mustn't lose our sense of humor. We have a secret weapon: no alternative. We have to fight. We have to win. Otherwise we are lost. The only friendly neighbor we have is the Mediterranean, and we are standing with our backs up to the sea."

The others nodded. So be it.

The decision was made to declare statehood on Friday, May 14, at four o'clock in the afternoon to avoid violating the Sabbath. But although she had contributed so valiantly and tirelessly to the creation of the state, Golda was to be unable to witness the ceremony! For once, her rigid self-discipline and devotion to duty nearly deserted her. Just one day before the proclamation, on Thursday, May 13, she must return to Jerusalem and remain at her post there. Heavy-hearted, Golda went to the airport and took off in the "primus."

But "good luck" in the form of engine trouble interceded, and every detail of that hair-raising trip remained grooved in her memory:

"As the plane reached the Judean Hills, the motor began to knock in an abnormal way, and we were afraid that we would lose it completely. I sat next to the pilot—there was no other place. The plane carried only two people. I noticed that the pilot was very nervous. Naturally, I did not want to show him that I was concerned, too. The pilot told me, 'I'm sorry, but I don't think that I will be able to clear the mountains. I shall have to return.'

"Now, it's impossible to argue with the pilot if he feels that he cannot continue; that's his profession. The plane turned around, and then the motor began to knock in an even more ominous fashion. I noticed that the pilot was looking around below. Again I did not say anything. After a while, the motor picked up a bit and he asked me: 'Do you know what is happening?'

" 'Yes,' I replied.

" 'I was looking,' he continued, 'for the most likely Arab village where we could land.' And this was May thirteenth! 'But,' he added, 'now I think I shall put down in Ben Shemen.' The motor improved a bit just then. 'No,' he said, 'I think we can make it back to Tel Aviv.' "

And that was how Golda Meyerson was able to be present at the ceremony next day!

David Ben-Gurion called a special session of the Jewish National Council in the Museum of Modern Art in Tel Aviv and announced "the establishment of the Jewish state in Palestine to be called Israel." The Jewish people had condensed thirty-four centuries of their history into thirty-four minutes, and a nation was reborn!

One by one the Jewish leaders signed the proclamation, and then it was Golda Meyerson's turn, one of the two women to share this great honor. Her emotions were so turbulent that all she could ever remember of the occasion was a feeling of awe at being privileged to participate and that David Pincus, one of the signers, came over to her and tried to comfort her because she was weeping uncontrollably.

That night in the synagogues of the state of Israel, this text from Amos 9:11, 14–15, was read:

> I will bring back the captives of my people Israel . . . and I will plant them upon their land, and they shall no more be plucked out of their land which I have given them, says the Lord your God.

CHAPTER 13

"The Most Passionate Zionist Speech I Have Ever Heard!"

ON THE DIPLOMATIC front the state of Israel's first victory was its immediate recognition by President Harry S Truman. For Golda, recalling her youth in America, this act of a great and modest President was especially meaningful, and it seemed to her that it would go down in Israel's history as one of its brightest landmarks. But victory—or defeat—on the military front loomed as a very large question indeed.

The day the proclamation was signed Golda stayed overnight in Tel Aviv, and a number of Haganah leaders came to see her.

"They are massing on the borders," the military men told her. "There is no doubt that they will cross tonight."

On Saturday morning, May 15, at 5:30, Golda watched two related happenings through the window of her hotel room: the first Egyptian air raid and the arrival of a ship with refugees who did not have visas and who did not now need them, for they were coming home to the state of Israel.

The next day, Golda received a cable from the head of the United Jewish Appeal in the United States suggesting that she return to America as quickly as possible, because he thought she could raise another $50 million in the wake of American Jewry's elation over the proclamation of

113

statehood. She dearly wished she could remain in Israel and share its first joys and sorrows, but like a devoted Jewish mother, she wrenched herself away from the three-day-old infant to see what she could do in this life-or-death emergency to help keep it alive.

The Arab League's invasion timetable called for Lebanon and Syria to attack from the north, Iraq and Trans-Jordan from the east, and Egypt from the south. Supremely confident of their overwhelming advantages in numbers and armament, the invaders had little reason during the first weeks to doubt that they would bring off the invasion on schedule.

Israel's weakest position was in Jerusalem. King Abdullah's superbly trained Arab Legion under its expatriate British commander, Glubb Pasha, was shelling without letup. Daily he bombarded the modern sector outside the walls, where the bulk of the city's 100,000 Jews lived. The legion isolated Jerusalem from the rest of the country and cut off its supply route by holding Latrun, midway between Jerusalem and Tel Aviv. The plan was to shell and to starve the Israelis into submission. The shells rained alike on public buildings, homes, and civilians in the streets. Casualties were enormous, estimated at five times those of London under the Nazi blitz. Most terrible of all was the plight of some 2,500 aged Jewish scholars in the Old City who were cut off from the main Jewish area.

But the people did not live up to Arab expectations—they refused to break under the punishment.

Regina Hamburger Medzini lived through the siege of Jerusalem with her husband and two children, and her experience was typical:

"Our water ration went down to a glass a day. We had a daily food ration of four olives and a piece of bread. I lost twenty-two pounds during the siege, and ever since then, I, and everyone else who knew the hunger of those days, will never leave anything on our plates. Yet life can be very simple under stress. We had no electricity, so when the city went dark, we all went to bed. Believe it or not, no one got sick, or at least no one admitted to being sick. Every one of us went to work without missing a day."

What was far less endurable was their inability to fight back. "To have to sit helplessly while the Arabs cannonaded the city day after day and night after night in the knowledge that we had no comparable cannon with which to hit back was worse than any other hardship."

But members of the Palmach secretly cleared a rough track through the mountains, following a goat path. A human chain of two hundred volunteers, mostly men over fifty years old, carried forty-five-pound sacks of flour on their backs over the three-mile stretch to the Jerusalem road. Making two trips a night for five nights, this human chain helped at least to alleviate the most acute hunger of some of the people under siege.

The best allies the Israelis had were the overconfidence, faulty coordination, and animosity among the leaders of the Arab forces and the low morale and lack of incentive among the rank-and-file soldiers.

In the north the Syrians were blocked by the do-or-die determination of the kibbutzim. The Egyptian advance from the south was stalled by the dug-in fighters of the Jewish settlements in the Negev, which, although isolated, were being supplied by planes at night.

A month after the hostilities had begun, the Security Council of the United Nations stepped in and ordered a cease-fire. A four-week truce, beginning June 11, was negotiated by the United Nations mediator, Count Folke Bernadotte, of Sweden.

The truce provided the Israelis with a breathing spell which they put to excellent advantage. Under the inspired leadership of a New York–born West Point graduate,

Colonel David (Mickey) Marcus, who volunteered his services to Israel, an incredible feat of engineering—a "Burma Road"—was built which bypassed Latrun and permitted convoys of supplies and arms to reach the besieged Jews of Jerusalem.

The Israel Defense Army, augmented by large numbers of refugees who had streamed into the country and who had been intensively trained by the Haganah, now had heavy armaments. When the Arabs refused to extend the truce, the Israelis took the offensive and captured key towns to such effect that after ten days of fighting, the Arabs agreed to another truce. And when, in mid-October, fighting erupted in the south, the Israelis smashed the Egyptian line, and the Negev settlements were relieved.

In New York Golda received a cable from the Israeli Government, asking her to accept an appointment as ambassador to Moscow. To her the appointment meant exile, and she was most reluctant to accept it. But she understood how important it was to acknowledge the Soviet Union's recognition of the state of Israel by establishing diplomatic relations as quickly as possible. If Ben-Gurion thought her best qualified for the post, then she must accept it.

A few days before she was to leave for Israel, Golda was hospitalized with a broken leg sustained in a taxi accident. The leg was slow to mend, and phlebitis (inflammation of the veins), which still plagues her, set in. Ben-Gurion cabled: "When can you take over?" adding still another reason for Golda to be impatient with her slow recovery. Like all public figures, she had her critics, and they began to circulate reports that Golda was reluctant to go to Moscow and that was why she was "lingering on" at the hospital. Deeply hurt, Golda's patience ran out, and she left the hospital before her physicians thought it safe to do so.

Back again in Israel, Golda set about choosing a staff for her embassy in Moscow and concerning herself with the minutiae of diplomatic protocol, which was unfamiliar territory to her and to the other government officials of the infant state, so she had to rely heavily on improvisation.

As personal aides, Golda chose two extremely capable women. One of them was Eiga Shapiro, an old friend and contemporary, who had emigrated to Palestine from Poland two years earlier than Golda, in 1919. She was a most personable gentlewoman of great taste and refinement and with a wide range of experience as a private secretary to Dr. Chaim Weizmann and with the Jewish Agency. Her other choice was charming and witty Lou Kadar, a younger woman, born in France, who had come to Palestine in 1935. Since diplomacy was multilingual, she would serve as French interpreter and secretary.

While in New York, Golda had received a telegram from Israel asking whether she had any objection to having her daughter Sara accompany her to Moscow as the radio operator on her staff. Golda was delighted. She would never have asked for Sara's appointment, but she was very touched by the consideration being shown her.

Sara, then twenty-two, had fallen in love with a fellow kibbutznik at Revivim, a young Yemenite named Zacharia, who was also to go to Moscow as a code and radio expert. Before leaving Israel, Sara and Zacharia, a blend of eastern and western Jewry, were married in the garden of Shana's house in Holon with only a few intimates present.

Regina was there. As secretary to Israel's Foreign Minister, Moshe Sharett, and later to Abba Eban, she would soon be living the life of a cosmopolite in Paris, London, and New York.

Moshe Meyerson also attended, and it was fortunate that he was on hand to share his daughter's happiness because only three years later, in 1951, he died.

On their arrival in Moscow on September 3, 1948, and until a suitable embassy could be found, Ambassador Golda Meyerson and the twenty-one members of her staff stayed at the Hotel Metropole. During her residence there, the flag of Israel was flown from the roof.

"If only the Czar could have seen that!" Golda exclaimed.

According to protocol, Golda must present her credentials to the Soviet Government as shortly after her arrival as possible because until she did, the Israeli delegation would have no official existence. Proper attire for the occasion was prescribed for the men, but there were no precedents for women diplomats. The only other woman diplomat in Moscow was from India, and she always wore a sari. Golda settled on a long black dress and a string of pearls which Eiga Shapiro lent her. She also wore a hat, which was quite a concession, since Golda disliked hats and nearly always went bareheaded. A crisis developed when it was discovered that the men were expected to wear white gloves, but the women solved it by giving them theirs. The gloves were too small for the men to wear, so they carried them instead and nonchalantly tossed them into their hats in passing them to the butler.

Within a couple of months the Israelis located a house which would serve as the embassy with a yard containing a few small buildings providing flats for the personnel. The house and the flats had to be furnished with everything from dustcloths on up, and the fact that no one knew just how much the Government could afford to spend did not make things easier. Eiga Shapiro was sent to Sweden and Denmark to buy what was necessary, since little in the way of goods was available in Moscow.

Eiga had a long shopping list—furniture, warm clothing, tinned food, and accessories for the entire staff. Since the Israelis had no diplomatic pouches, which are used to transmit official correspondence, when Eiga left on her mission, she put official letters in her suitcase and tied it with string; later she had Israel's first pouch designed in a Stockholm department store.

Many countries did not yet officially recognize Israel, but members of the various embassies came to the Israelis to pay their personal respects to Golda—"nicely and politely," she reported to her staff. Golda instituted Friday night open house at her embassy, which was a very popular event, particularly among newsmen, who rarely had any other place where they could relax informally.

Golda ran the embassy in kibbutz fashion; all members of her staff, including the cook and chauffeur, sat down to meals together, and all were given equal amounts of pocket money. And this meant *all*—for Golda insisted on the same arrangement for herself. She also insisted, whenever possible, in doing some of the cooking and marketing herself, as well as little household chores, although the embassy had five Russian servants supervised by Hans, the Israeli chef, who did not know a word of the language.

On the first Shabbat after she had presented her credentials, Golda requested her staff to accompany her to the Moscow synagogue. Although neither she nor most of the others were Orthodox, she felt it appropriate to make this gesture toward the Jewish community. There were an estimated 500,000 Jews in Moscow, but Soviet repression had been so effective that only a few hundred worshipers were in attendance at services. Golda had announced her visit in advance only to the rabbi, but when her presence became known, all eyes turned toward her.

A few weeks later, on Rosh Hashanah, and again with no previous announcement, Golda decided to attend the services. Normally, even on the High Holy Days, only about two thousand persons attended services, but outside the synagogue Golda found herself engulfed by a crowd of 40,000 Russian Jews, in a spontaneous demonstration which jammed the entire area. A picture was taken of the scene, showing Golda's head just appearing in a sea of admirers. Evidently, hundreds of prints were made because, as Lou

1

0 SHALOM, GOLDA

Soviet Jews greet Israel's ambassador on Rosh Hashanah, September, 1948, at the Moscow synagogue.
(Photo: Zionist Archives and Library, New York)

Kadar reported, people would pass by her as she walked on a crowded Moscow street and whisper, "I've got the picture!"

Golda was profoundly moved. She felt the love they bore for her, perhaps not so much as a person but as a symbol of Israel. She remarked to Lou: "If an Israeli broomstick had appeared in their midst, these Russian Jews would have acclaimed it."

In accordance with Orthodox custom Golda and the other Israeli women sat upstairs in the segregated women's section of the synagogue. All through the service, people came up to them, touching them and then quietly going away.

Some asked about relatives in Israel; others kissed Golda's shoulder.

Again on Yom Kippur, Golda came, and by the time the congregation reached the prayer *l'shana habaah b'Yerushalaim*—"next year in Jerusalem"—the voices shook the synagogue, and all eyes were raised to Golda.

Golda said, through tears, "This is the most passionate Zionist speech I have ever heard."

Apparently, the Soviet Government had failed in more than thirty years of effort to wipe out Zionist sympathies among Russian Jewry.

"The privilege and heartbreaking experience I had with Soviet Jewry," Golda said later, "made me more certain of the survival of Soviet Jewry than I am of Jewry in some free countries. Not because that Jewry is better, but because I think that throughout our history it has been proven that outside forces, no matter how brutal, cannot force the Jews to stop being Jews. The only ones who can decide on assimilation, and assimilate, are Jews themselves, of their own free will."

Her sorrow for the silent, repressed Jews of Russia cut very deeply. Nor could she believe it a coincidence that in January, 1949, only five months after the demonstration outside the Moscow synagogue, the Soviet Government took a new series of repressive measures: The Jewish newspaper and publishing press were closed down, and the Yiddish theater was also banned.

"Somehow these Soviet Jews will come to us in Israel one day," Golda said. "One day it *will* happen."

Although she felt that in the main she was succeeding in her task of furthering friendly relations between the Soviet Union and Israel, she was not happy with her assignment. Protocol and the glamour surrounding her position meant very little to her. She ached to return to Israel and turn her energies loose there. An uneasy peace with the Arabs had come about. Count Bernadotte had been assassinated in Jerusalem by fanatic Jewish terrorists, and Dr. Ralph J. Bunche, who in 1951 became the highest-ranking American at the United Nations, had replaced him as mediator. At a neutral meeting place on the island of Rhodes in the Mediterranean, Israeli and Egyptian representatives had hammered out an armistice agreement. Jordan, Lebanon, and Syria had also worked out similar agreements. The War of Independence had been won. So much needed to be done to build the state of Israel, but Golda was still obliged to remain in Moscow!

In January, 1949, Israel held its first elections, and in February Golda was offered the cabinet post of Minister of Labor. She flew to Israel to take the oath of office with the other members of Israel's first elected government, then returned to Moscow to say her formal farewells.

At last, on April 20, 1949, she wound up her affairs at the embassy, hugged Sara and Zacharia, who would remain in Moscow for eight months, and took off for Israel and what she would always look upon as the "most productive years of my life."

"Let's Have <u>More</u> Jews!"

As THERE HAD never been a Ministry of Labor in Israel, Golda's first task was to establish one. Setting up the various departments and administrative procedures and enlisting technical experts to help formulate and execute her programs were among the problems she faced. Her personal supervision was felt everywhere. Each department head was required to visit her periodically and make a progress report, to which she listened intently. She then asked searching questions about the program under discussion to determine whether it was absolutely essential. Massive problems confronted her, and she could not include non-essential activities among her priorities.

"I do not," she said, "wish to be a Minister of Superfluous Affairs."

The first act of the Provisional Council after the Proclamation of Independence had been to rescind the British White Paper of 1939. In its place was the Law of Return, which stated that Aliyah, immigration to Israel, was an inherent privilege bestowed automatically upon every Jew, and indeed it was a basic purpose of the state. Every Jew who wished had the right to enter Israel and be granted citizenship simply by declaring his desire to settle there.

As Golda took office, immigrants were arriving in Israel by the hundreds of thousands, and she decided that her primary emphasis must be on how to absorb these new citizens rather than on such standard labor items as hours of work, wages, or, as she said, "water coolers in the factories." During her first two years as Minister of Labor, immigration peaked to 685,000, more than doubling the population of Israel.

One of the more remarkable examples of Aliyah and one that created very complex problems was the Yemenite immigration during 1949 and 1950, which became known as Operation Magic Carpet. Jews had lived in Yemen, in southwest Arabia, from before the second destruction of the Temple in A.D. 70. They still wore long robes, silver-fringed hoods, prayer shawls, and lovelocks, as they had in biblical days. Although they lived among Arabs and spoke Arabic, the men all studied Hebrew and knew the Bible intimately. Like the monks of the Middle Ages, they copied the Old Testament by hand on beautiful scrolls, and each day they prayed: "Next year, Oh Lord, in Jerusalem." Only their intense religious fervor could have sustained them through poverty, disease, and persecution. When they learned that now, with the creation of the state of Israel, their prayer could be answered, an exodus of forty thousand to fifty thousand Yemenites began.

The imam of Yemen required them to leave behind whatever little property they had and to pay a head tax for each person, including infants in arms, who wished to leave. Crammed into hired trucks, they drove to San'a, the capital city, and then down the mountains to the Aden border, paying ransom to each sultan or sheikh along the way until they reached the Joint Distribution Committee camp in the desert some thirteen miles out of Aden. At the camp they received their first bread and water after riding all day and half the night; children were given milk and a blanket against the cold desert night. In the morning they were deloused with disinfectant spray, allowed to bathe,

Young refugees at a Yemenite tent camp near Jerusalem

and given new clothes and Israel identity cards. Trucks
then transported them to the airfield for the flight to Israel
in old American C-54 Skymasters whose conventional fit-
tings had been ripped out and replaced with benches to ac-
commodate a maximum planeload of 140 passengers. The
sixteen-hundred-mile flight took eight and a half hours over

the shark-infested waters of the Gulf of Aden and up the Red Sea. There were no navigation guides except the ships below, and a forced landing in any of the Arab countries would mean disaster. In this manner, from the summer of 1949 on, about five hundred Yemenite families were landing at Lydda airport near Tel Aviv each day.

All the "ten plagues of Yemen," the results of poverty, afflicted them: tuberculosis, trachoma, ringworm, malaria, anemia, typhoid, dysentery, measles, toxicity, and pellagra. Hospitals and clinics were opened overnight, many by Hadassah, under the supervision of the Israel Ministry of Health. At first they were settled into tent camps. In one Hadassah project alone, near Jerusalem, thirteen thousand Yemenites lived in a tent city. Frightened children had to be made to feel secure enough to play and sing again. Mothers were instructed in breast-feeding their babies hygienically and in diapering them, for they had never used diapers before. The cots provided for them were considered great luxuries: They had never slept in beds.

As she saw it, Golda's task was to resettle these immigrants into villages and farms as soon as possible and to set them to work in the orange groves and public-works projects, especially road-building. Israel was a country almost without roads or with roads that were cut off at arbitrary points by the partition boundaries. It was impossible, for example, to reach the Dead Sea because existing roads went through the Jordanian part of Jerusalem.

Some economists felt that large-scale housing and public-works programs were "nonproductive" at this stage and that the state's limited funds were best directed into agriculture and industry. It would be cheaper, they argued, to give immigrants a dole and take care of their housing and job needs later on.

Golda utterly disagreed. What could be more nonproductive in the long run than demoralization of Israel's new citizens by a dole?

"It is my contention," she said, "that good citizenship and decent behavior cannot develop as long as people live in tents. There is no sense in talking about social responsibility and duty to the country as long as the immigrants live in abominable physical conditions. Nor am I impressed by all the talk of delinquency among the immigrants. If my children had been hungry, I would have stolen bread for them. The economists forget that a man is a human being, not a statistical figure."

The burdens she shouldered would have crushed most people far younger than she.

"Golda doesn't think in terms of *hours* of work or 'I've finished my day's work,'" her legal adviser, Zvi Bar-Niv said of her. "She never closes the circle; it's always wide open. Working with her, we were all suicidal self–slave drivers."

One of the advantages of working with Golda was that if she believed in a person, she gave him full rein; otherwise the person could not work with her at all. Yet for all her hard work, efficiency, and dedication, there had to be a personal element in her dealings with people. Social values got built in; one could always speak to her as a friend, since she had the uncommon ability of putting people at ease with her from the first moment.

Some of her technical experts like Bar-Niv became worried and impatient. What would happen to all the fine plans for unemployment insurance, social security—all the programs he was supposed to be concerned with as legal adviser to the Ministry of Labor? He nudged Golda about going ahead with the program of long-range social legislation instead of dealing personally with the unemployment problem.

He told her: "You're doing the work of a whole fire brigade. What about your future reputation?"

"As long as the unemployed are demonstrating before my ministry," Golda said, "I don't have time to deal with things relating to my future reputation or image."

He was given no choice. He must help her deal with housing and unemployment, and then in due time they would get around to the long-range goals.

As an interim step to providing permanent housing for the new immigrants, Golda stepped up the program of building ma'abarot, or transit work villages, in which the people were housed in single-room huts prefabricated out of corrugated iron, aluminum, or canvas. In these huts, even though their quarters might be overcrowded and shared with chickens, there were such amenities as a cupboard and a stove instead of a campfire. But her goal was the construction of whole villages of permanent concrete bungalows, situated near places of employment, on the outskirts of cities, and in areas of industrial development. This dispersion was an integral part of Golda's plan to prevent the formation of city ghettos and to put workers near jobs.

To get a massive housing program moving, Golda had to prod and bully workers in the construction trades to pitch in, even though it might entail a financial sacrifice. Also, she was keenly aware of the fact that some established Israelis found the alien cultures of the Yemenite, Iraqi, and Egyptian Jews repugnant and looked down on them because of their extremely low standard of living.

Golda did not spare them: "We are all feeling the heat," she told a workers' delegation in July, 1950. "But I already feel next winter's cold because I tremble at every warm summer day that passes and brings us closer to the days of rain and storms and perhaps even snow as well. Yet ten skilled building workers to put up houses in Acre and another ten for Halsa and another five for somewhere else and another ten for Beersheba—they're not to be had."

She told them that she saw only one purpose for a Jewish state: to hold the gates of Israel wide open to immigrants without any restrictions, and if suffering resulted, then everybody should suffer together.

"I'm prepared," she said, and they believed her, "to go not only from meeting to meeting but from door to door so that every single one of us may realize that when he sits at a table, when he puts on a suit, when he makes improvements on his house, does something for his child, he is doing it at the expense of all of us. Let's see how we'll enjoy life with this realization. For this is the truth."

By the end of 1950 ma'abarot had largely replaced tent camps, and by May, 1951, a network of these work villages began to cover the country, ending the first phase of immigrant absorption. Now Golda moved on to the next stage, which was more permanent housing.

"Let's have *more* problems of absorption of Jews," Golda exulted. "If anybody knows in the first place what it means to be a refugee and in the second place how to solve a refugee problem, we are tops. After all, we *are* a refugee people!"

She had her wish. Iraq announced that the ninety thousand Jews who wished to leave the country for Israel must do so by May 31, 1951. Iraq was technically still at war with Israel and would not permit a direct flight between the two countries. But the deadline was met. This largest of airlifts flew the Iraqi Jews to Cyprus, where they were transferred to other aircraft, even though this meant a detour of several hundred miles and increased both the cost of the flights and the number of planes needed.

"Golda-on-the-Spot," as she was now being nicknamed, had to see for herself what was going on. At least one full day a week, Golda visited the immigrant villages, inspected housing projects and roads, and met with students at the vocational centers.

Whenever her associates begged her to slow down, she refused even to consider it. "You can't work here in the office," the fifty-two-year-old minister insisted, "if you don't work in the field."

She was everywhere, requesting, demanding, suggesting. Golda learned that there was dissatisfaction with architects' plans for a housing project for a new town, Kiryat Shemona, near the Lebanon border. She toured the site and saw that the plans called for one steep step from the kitchen door to the ground.

"Oh, no!" Golda told the engineers. "How would you like your wife to jump forty centimeters to the ground every time she wanted to empty the garbage pail?"

She insisted that some other way be found to cut costs, and the houses were built with two steps outside the kitchen door.

On another occasion Golda attended the opening ceremony for a new road to an Israeli Arab village, and she made a speech about the function of roads in uniting people and helping them to communicate. For the first time Arab women, heartened by Golda's presence, attended a public meeting.

One woman, more daring than the rest, even spoke up. "To make us a road is very kind of you," she told Golda. "But roads and cars are for men. We women still have to carry water pails on our heads from the floor of the valley up to the mountain."

Listening, as always, Golda took the cue, and water pipes were laid at the same time that work on the road progressed. Main arteries were constructed as well as approach roads which connected settlements and opened up new areas for settlement and development. Instead of a dole, which was anathema to Golda except for disabled persons, the aged, or dependent children, her ministry was providing about seven million workdays per year on constructive and permanent undertakings, such as radio stations, electric power plants, and bridges, as well as houses and roads.

She was unimpressed when economists offered statistics demonstrating that for the most part Israelis were fairly well housed and employed.

"Every unemployed man or woman is one hundred percent unemployed," she said. "Every family that lacks decent housing is one hundred percent miserable. Economic problems are not problems of numbers but problems of flesh and blood—human problems."

The large-scale absorption of immigrants meant that Israelis would have to accept a rigorous austerity program if they were to maintain an unrestricted flow of immigration. By December, 1951, the only unrationed staple foods in the whole of Israel were bread, cream cheese, leben (a milk food similar to yogurt), and frozen fish fillets. Practically everything else—meat, chicken, fresh fish, flour, sugar, coffee, tea, tomatoes, green peppers, all fats and oils (including washing and toilet soap), potatoes, eggs—were stringently rationed.

A letter from a housewife, which appeared in one of the Israeli newspapers, reflected the general public view:

> Yes, rationing and immigrants; we can have them both or neither and there's no hesitancy on that score at all. The sands are running out fast in Iraq, Romania, and Algiers. Day after day, the immigrants come in with a flood that almost inundates us with problems and risks. Everything is challenged: standard of living, state of health, culture, economic position, even morals. Have we got the guts to face it?

From the vast majority of Israelis, the answer was, "Yes, we can!"

But even the austerity programs were inadequate to meet the needs of a newly developing country that was nearly drowning in the flood of immigrants.

"My ministry," Golda sighed, "not only has to present a program and execute it. Into the bargain it has to raise the needed capital."

So she was off to America as a "schnorrer" yet again, to persuade American Jewry to help provide the wherewithal for the long-term needs of the new state.

But Golda was a proud, even imperious schnorrer. At one of the meetings of American Jews she attended, a man asked her, "What about packages to Israel?"

Golda took a deep breath. "Now, this maybe seems funny to you," she replied, "but it is not funny to me. I am a citizen of Israel, and I absolutely refuse to be classified as someone belonging to a people whose needs can be answered by packages."

She preferred, rather, the approach of the National Planning Conference for Israel and Jewish Rehabilitation to which she was a delegate where ways and means were explored to "uphold the hands of Israel" in making absorption of immigration and development of the country possible. The incredible sum of $1 billion was to be raised by American Jewry, and a portion of this sum was to be contributed by Israel over a three-year period.

As security for Israel's debt, Golda offered "thousands and thousands of children of Israel, the children of old-timers, and the little Yemenite children and Iraqi children and the Romanian children and children from all over the world, many of whom are bewildered because they can walk around free in the streets of our country."

By 1953 Golda's ministry had implemented the construction of 82,000 flats with two rooms and kitchenette in permanent concrete buildings, including groceries, synagogues, and schools to service the projects; 1,200 public buildings; and 52,000 temporary housing units.

Now she felt she could pay closer attention to the long-range programs. She presented to the Knesset (Israel's parliament) the National Insurance Bill, which was basic to the concept of a socialist state that she had held ever since she had joined the Labor Zionists at the age of seventeen, and it was unanimously adopted in November, 1953.

In presenting the bill Golda called attention to it as a historic turning point in Israel's social development:

"The state of Israel which has risen to independence will not tolerate within it poverty which shames human life; it will not tolerate within it the possibility that the happiest hour of a mother's life will be marred by worry and poverty. The state of Israel will not tolerate within it the possibility that men and women who reach old age will curse the day of their birth. They will live out their old age in happiness, assured that the country which they have served through their work over many years knows how to support them when they are old. In the knowledge that this is only a first step, I want to congratulate the entire Knesset on this proud day."

Of special concern to Golda was the high infant-mortality rate among new immigrants and Arab women. To encourage them to give birth in hospitals, the bill provided for maternity benefits covering hospitalization costs plus a sum for the baby. One of her joyous tasks was to hand over, personally, the first check to the first Arab woman to deliver her baby in the hospital at Nazareth.

Golda's ministry was also responsible for writing a code of labor laws for Israel. "It is the Jewish people that first carved out the path of ethics, of many fundamental ethical values, including concern for the worker," she said in the Knesset, "for his rest, his wages, the conditions of his work. We have continued in this tradition."

In addition, Golda sponsored a Woman's Labor Act, banning night work and occupations harmful to women, instituting a twelve-week maternity leave, at least half of it after childbirth (at 75 percent of full pay), and prohibiting the dismissal of pregnant women or women on maternity leave without the consent of the Ministry of Labor.

Another crucial necessity was to develop vocational education for both adults and young people. Before World War II 57 percent of the immigrants had been skilled workers, but in the first few years of statehood this figure dropped to 15 percent as mass immigration brought men and women from Europe's ghettos who had no trades or professions and the people of the East who were largely unskilled and penniless.

Golda's program called for the recruitment of skilled factory personnel as teachers, rental of lofts as workshops, and enrollment of students from the refugee camps. Not only were the vocational centers free, but the students were given a subsidy to finance them while studying. At first the dropout rate was over 25 percent, but it soon decreased to 5 percent and remained at that level while the number of courses expanded to 160 subjects. By the end of 1952 some thirty thousand immigrants had been taught special trades and crafts.

Always deeply concerned with young people, Golda persuaded parents of teen-agers who were unsuited to academic pursuits to send them into vocational programs, and many of these young people turned out to be the best technicians in the Israel Defense Army.

Young people were also recruited into agricultural programs, and at least one experience epitomized for Golda what all her tremendous effort was directed toward.

A former police station overlooking the sea had been built by the British as a lookout to spot and prevent the landing of illegal immigrants during the White Paper period. Now the police station was being used for a regional conference of young people engaged in poultry-breeding.

As Golda walked across an iron bridge to visit the station,

she told her companions: "Anyone who is depressed by our present difficulties should recall the heavy lead in our hearts as we walked over the bridges connecting the prison camps on Cyprus, where forty thousand of our people awaited a safe landing on these very shores. The conference in progress at the police station today should lift our spirits with the pride of accomplishment since the birth of the state."

In just a few years of its existence the state had come a long way, and Golda had traveled along every foot of it. But the state—and Golda, who was such an integral part of it —had only turned a corner.

CHAPTER 15

"Golda Is the Best Man in My Cabinet"

By 1956 it was apparent that Israel, for the second time, would have to fight for her life against the neighboring Arab states which refused to recognize her right to exist in their midst and whose leaders, largely indifferent to the welfare of their own people, diverted their best energies to the single end of pushing the Israelis into the sea.

The fedayeen, armed Arab guerrillas, had Egypt's blessings to raid Israeli settlements, kill and wound civilians, and commit acts of sabotage. In 1952 Colonel Gamal Abdel Nasser had headed a military coup which overthrew King Farouk of Egypt. As head of government he had signed an arms agreement with Czechoslovakia for quantities of Soviet-made planes, tanks, and guns and for Soviet instructors to teach the Egyptians how to use them. To take the guesswork out of what these military preparations signified, Radio Cairo, in almost daily broadcasts, blared:

"The day of Israel's destruction approaches. This is our decision and this is our faith. There shall be no peace on the borders, for we demand vengeance, and vengeance means death to Israel."

How to deal with the Arab threat had caused a breach between Prime Minister Ben-Gurion and his Foreign Minister, Moshe Sharett, and in June, 1956, it came out into the open, with most of the members of the cabinet, including Golda, siding with Ben-Gurion and his more aggressive

Golda served in every Israeli cabinet since statehood. Here she is with President Itzhak Ben-Zvi (sitting to her left) and Prime Minister Moshe Sharett (on Ben-Zvi's left) in 1954.

stance toward retaliation for Arab guerrilla attacks. When, shortly afterward, Sharett resigned, Ben-Gurion asked Golda to replace him.

To be asked to take over as Foreign Minister, the second most important post in the Government, at a time of grave crisis reflected Ben-Gurion's enormous regard and respect for Golda's abilities.

"Golda," Ben-Gurion said, "is the best man in my cabinet."

But she was less than elated. During her seven years as Minister of Labor she had seen the tangible results of her programs in greater human happiness. Much still remained to be done, and she ardently wished she could see more of her projects through to completion. The Foreign Ministry, she felt, offered no such rewards. Her experience as ambassador to Moscow had shown her that she had little taste for formal receptions and dinners or for protocol, which she described as "all that hocus-pocus." Also, she was happiest when living in Israel, in close contact with her children and grandchildren. She did not relish the life of a Foreign Minister who must often be away either at the United Nations in New York or traveling the world.

Yet she placed Israel's welfare over any personal considerations, and if she could best serve the state as its Foreign Minister, then she must serve.

Only a few months after she had taken office, the threat of war was so unmistakable that Israel's very existence hung precariously in the balance. The armistice that the Arabs and Jews had signed ending the 1948–1949 War of Independence clearly provided that "no aggressive action by the armed forces—land, sea, or air—of either Party shall be undertaken, planned, or threatened against the people or armed forces of the other." But the Arabs continued to insist that a state of war still existed, and in July Egypt barred Israel from the Suez Canal and the Strait of Tiran, which was her waterway to the East.

Then, on October 24, 1956, Egypt announced that a military pact had been signed with Jordan and Syria, which placed all their forces under the unified command of Egypt, and that the pact "represented a supreme effort to tighten the death noose around Israel." Information was also received that the training of 2,500 fedayeen at three bases in the Sinai was now virtually completed, and they were to be deployed among the three Arab countries to launch all-out marauding attacks against the Israelis from the north, south, and center.

Israel's Chief of Staff, Brigadier General Moshe Dayan, other top military leaders, Ben-Gurion, Golda, and a few other key members of the Government met and finalized secret plans to forestall an invasion by a surprise attack. Golda, for one, had no doubts whatsoever over the correctness of the decision to attack first:

"If we wait for Nasser to attack, someone in the United Nations eventually will make a speech about the nice little people that don't exist anymore," she said wryly. "I suppose that if we allow ourselves to be killed off piecemeal by Nasser, or to wait until he chooses the day to exterminate all of us in one attack, we will be wept over and eulogized. No people in the world knows about collective eulogies as much as we Jews do. Six million killed in one generation, out of a people of eighteen millions, we consider quite sufficient."

The attack was set for Monday, October 29. On the Friday before, Golda went to Revivim to visit Sara and her children. As Golda knew very well, if the Egyptian forces ever reached the Negev, Sara's kibbutz would be one of the first to be overrun. Yet she could not warn Sara because she was pledged to absolute secrecy. But as she was leaving, the young man in charge of kibbutz security took Golda aside and said he had heard of secret mobilization orders.

"I'm not asking any questions," he said, "but do you think we should dig ditches?"

Golda nodded. "If I were you, I would."

The Israel Defense Army was so geared as to be able to mobilize in two or three days. Military service was compulsory for all eighteen-year-old boys and girls except those who were married or asked for exemption on religious grounds. Boys served for twenty-six months and girls for twenty months. All branches—army, air force, and navy—were under a single General Staff and one Chief of Staff; all ranks had the same names in all the services.

The draftees were the full-time army in uniform, and after their term of military service was over, they were attached to reserve units which trained for one month each year. The girls were not assigned to combat but served as nurses, clerks, and signalers. Since they were often near the front lines, they were taught to use rifles, hand grenades, and submachine guns. Protecting the new settlements close to the borders were young men and girls recruited from the various youth movements into what were called Nahal units, which combined military service with settling, cultivating, and protecting the land. On orders to mobilize, this citizens' army left the stores, factories, farms, and universities and went down to their posts in public buses, taxis, and milk trucks.

The Sinai Campaign, under the command of Brigadier General Moshe Dayan has since been called one of the most brilliant strategies in military annals. By tactical surprise, skilled use of air power and parachute troops, and swift maneuverability of infantry and armor, the Israelis routed the Egyptians in four days—or one hundred hours—of fighting. The Israelis occupied the Sinai Peninsula, which is three times the size of Israel, and the Gaza Strip, a small section of Palestine which the Egyptian forces had occupied in 1948. They opened a sea route through the Gulf of 'Aqaba from their southern port of Elath, bypassing the Suez Canal as a link with Africa and Asia.

Golda left strategy to the generals and interpreted the victory in the human terms in which she saw everything.

"Our army," she said, "has one thing that you cannot buy for money. Nor can you get it as a present from the big powers. This is a thing that either one has in one's heart and soul or one hasn't. That is the spirit, the conviction of justice. It was the ammunition that our people took with them into the Sinai Desert, just as they did in 1948—and again they came back victorious."

She pointed out that two philosophies had clashed in the desert: Whereas Israeli soldiers carried copies of the Bible in their knapsacks, many Egyptian soldiers carried Arabic translations of Hitler's *Mein Kampf* in theirs. In that case, were not the Israelis bound to win?

The United Nations Security Council ordered a cease-fire on November 1. A little over a month later, on December 5, 1956, Golda Meyerson, who was now Golda Meir (having Hebraized her name as requested by Ben-Gurion), made her debut in a full-scale address to the General Assembly, eliciting unusual interest because she was the world's only woman Foreign Minister.

She described how in 1948, twelve hours after the state of Israel was proclaimed, Egyptian bombers attacked Tel Aviv, yet the United Nations had neither helped Israel nor acted against the aggressors, and how, that same day, the first Jewish refugee ships from camps in Germany arrived in Israel.

"These two episodes," she said, "are symbolic of the life of Israel since its inception—rescue and reconstruction, menaced constantly by the destructive efforts of its neighbors.

"Mr. President," she continued, "what ought to be done now? Are we in our relations with Egypt to go back to an armistice regime which has brought anything but peace and which Egypt derisively flouted? Shall the Sinai Desert again breed nests of fedayeen and of aggressive armies poised for the assault? Will certain countries rearm Egypt for the renewed pursuit of its announced aims? Must the tragedy be reenacted in the tinderbox of the Middle East?"

As it turned out, the answer to all her questions was Yes. Once again the aggressors who had lost the war obtained the upper hand over the defenders who had won, and the Arab bloc in the United Nations maneuvered the big powers into compelling Israel to withdraw from the Sinai Desert and the Gaza Strip, handing the area over for policing by a United Nations emergency force. In return, the maritime powers guaranteed the right of free passage for Israeli shipping in the Gulf of 'Aqaba.

Ever after, Golda looked upon her withdrawal speech of March 1, 1957, as the low point of her entire career.

"One of the things in my life that I'm not very proud of is the fact that I had to make the statement on behalf of my government . . . of our hopes and aspirations as we agreed to withdraw from the positions. I cannot even pride myself that it was I who made up this statement. Every word and every comma and every dot were cleared with the late Mr. Dulles [John Foster Dulles, then Secretary of State under President Dwight D. Eisenhower]. And he in turn cleared it with other maritime powers. It was only after the guarantees of the maritime powers and the United States that I got up and made the statement. . . . That was not my greatest hour."

As a bitter postscript to Israel's withdrawal, it was Colonel Nasser who erected a "victory" monument in the city of Gaza. As for Israel, she still had no peace treaty with the Arabs and no recognition of her existence as a state.

"To my sorrow," Golda told intimates, "one can easily become a cynic in the United Nations. We talk about equality, one country, one vote. But when they're looking around for a chairman or a new secretary, they look at the blocs of countries, African, Asian, or whatever. Poor little Israel with one little vote! What does she count?"

Year after year, the problem of Arab refugees was debated at the United Nations, and, year after year, Golda Meir answered the accusations of the Arab countries which charged Israel with responsibility for the hundreds of thousands of men, women, and children who were wasting their lives away in tent camps in hopelessness and despair.

"The Arabs know full well," Golda said, "that the refugee problem was of their own making when they launched war against Israel on the day of its birth."

Nor did she need to rely on her own statement of the facts. Arabs themselves had testified to what had really accounted for the problem of the Arab refugees in their own newspapers and periodicals.

Who had instigated the mass exodus of Palestine Arabs in the months preceding the outbreak of war in 1948?

Koul Shai, a weekly published in Lebanon, stated in August, 1951: "Who brought the Palestinians to the Lebanon as refugees? Who brought them over in dire straits and penniless? The Arab states, and Lebanon among them, did it."

A Jordanian daily, *Al-Urdun,* agreed and offered more detail: "For the flight and fall of the villages, it is our leaders who are responsible because of their dissemination of rumors exaggerating Jewish crime and describing them as atrocities in order to inflame the Arabs. By spreading rumors of Jewish atrocities, killings of women and children, they instilled fear and terror in the hearts of the Arabs in Palestine until they fled, leaving their homes and property to the enemy."

Of course, not all Arabs panicked and fled. Many thousands remained in Israel and continued to live peacefully and securely within the state. To those Arabs who remained, the behavior of their relatives and friends who ran seemed inexplicable.

But an explanation was offered in a report printed in *Falastin,* another Jordanian daily: "We the refugees who have brothers and friends among the Arabs of Israel have the right to address the members of the Arab League Council and declare: 'We left our homeland on the strength of false promises by crooked leaders in the Arab states. They promised us that our absence would not last more than two weeks, a kind of promenade, at the end of which we would return.' "

And still another Jordanian daily wistfully reported: "The Arab Governments told us: 'Get out so that we can get in!' So we got out, but they did not get in!"

Here were the facts as the Arab people themselves knew them to be, yet their leaders continued, by the familiar tactic of the "big lie," to deny them and haul Israel, like a criminal, before the bar of world opinion.

Israel's Foreign Minister could not be intimidated. Who knew better than she how Israel had dealt with the problem of Jewish refugees? Who had helped more than she, as Minister of Labor, to absorb them and build a new life for them, although it meant austerity and sacrifice for everyone?

"Compare this," she said, "with the Arab treatment of Arab refugees. Here are gigantic Arab territories with vast, underpopulated spaces and great unharnessed rivers for irrigation. The United Nations voted a fund of two hundred million dollars for Arab refugee resettlement. The Eric Johnston Jordan project of the United States Government would have provided homes for three hundred thousand Arab refugees. Israel, for its part, announced its readiness to compensate the refugees for the property they abandoned. All the conditions existed for the Arab Governments to solve this problem if they really wished to do so."

Why, then, she wanted to know, did the Arab refugee problem still plague the Middle East and the world? Why didn't the Arab Governments restore their kinsmen to a decent, productive life?

The answer was plain. "As a former representative of the United Nations relief organization said," she reminded her colleagues in the General Assembly, "they prefer to preserve the refugee camps as an open sore, as an affront against the United Nations and a weapon against Israel.

"Do you really want to know when the Arab refugee problem will be settled?" she added. "It will be when the Arabs love their children more than they hate us."

CHAPTER 16

Who Better Than a Jew Understands African Problems?

As FOREIGN MINISTER, along with Hebraizing her name to
Golda Meir, her whole life-style changed. She moved into
the large and rather splendid official residence in Jerusalem
which was guarded by two policemen. The ground floor,
with its large, handsomely decorated drawing room, dining
room, study, and huge kitchen, was designed for the formal
entertainment of foreign dignitaries, members of the diplomatic corps of other countries, artists, scholars, and other
distinguished guests.

On evenings when she entertained at formal dinners,
Golda left her office earlier than usual to check the table
setting, arrange the place cards supplied her by the protocol
section of her ministry, and make countless other last-
minute decisions.

"One of my friends once told me that my greatest short-
coming as a female Foreign Minister was that I didn't have
a wife to take care of all that for me," Golda laughed.
"Believe me, on particularly busy days, I was inclined to
agree with her!"

Her cherished private apartment was on the second floor
and had a small sitting room, a few bedrooms, and a little
kitchen. These rooms were furnished with her personal belongings—two walls of books, paintings by Israeli artists,
a Persian rug, a simple sofa with many chairs (almost all

bought secondhand) grouped around it, and a large coffee table, which she had found long ago in the Old City in Jerusalem. Always there were vases of fresh flowers and plants near the windows.

Neither of her children lived with her. Menahem, now aged thirty, had studied cello in the United States at the Manhattan School of Music in New York and with the great cellist Pablo Casals in Puerto Rico. He lived in Tel Aviv with his wife, Ayah, a psychiatrist, and their three children and taught at the Conservatory of Music. Sara, her husband, Zacharia, and their two children still lived at Revivim. So except for a housekeeper and maid who came in daily or for a student in residence, Golda lived in her big house all alone.

One of these students in residence, Ben Rabinovitsch, met the Foreign Minister casually on a street in Tel Aviv one day in 1960. His parents were friends of Golda's, and she had known him as a small boy. Ben told her that he had just recently finished his military service.

"What are you going to do now?" Golda asked.

Ben said that he was going to enroll in the Hebrew University in Jerusalem.

"If you haven't got a place to live yet," she said, aware of how scarce dormitory space was, "and if you like my house and think any of the rooms are suitable, you're welcome to stay with me."

Ben toured the official residence and settled into one of the servants' rooms, which, he knew, was far nicer than any he could have rented. One day he brought a young American girl friend to the house, and she was startled to see the splendor in which he was living.

"How come you live here?" she asked him.

Ben grinned. "Oh, that's to ensure the succession, to have the heir apparent here absorbing the ways of government!"

When he told Golda what he had said, she roared with laughter.

She still liked to cook whenever she had the chance and sometimes prepared supper for herself and Ben. He was in the kitchen one day while Golda stood at the sink peeling potatoes. One of the police guards came into the kitchen, saluted, and asked whether she needed anything done before he went off duty. The Foreign Minister wiped her hand on her apron, returned his salute, said, "No, thank you," then picked up her paring knife and started on another potato. It was Ben's turn to break into laughter, but Golda raised her eyebrows and asked, "What's so funny?"

Informality would always be her own personal style, and after she had held the post of Foreign Minister for a year or two, she became convinced that formal receptions, conversations, and diplomatic notes were not going to get Israel's message across to old or new countries. She decided to rely much more heavily on communication between human beings rather than between diplomats. Then she set out to travel the world, describing Israel's aspirations, achievements, and needs in simple terms and offering her own hand in friendship.

In February, 1958, Golda went off on her first African tour to the newly independent countries of Ghana, Nigeria, and the Ivory Coast, which was soon to receive its independence from France.

When asked about the nature of her feelings toward Africa, Golda referred to a passage in Theodor Herzl's book *Altneuland:*

> . . . there is still one other question arising out of the disaster of the nations which remains unsolved to this day, whose profound tragedy only a Jew can comprehend. That is the African question. Just call to mind all those terrible episodes of the slave trade, of human beings who merely because they were black were stolen like cattle, taken prisoner, captured and sold. Their children grew up in strange lands, the objects

> of contempt and hostility because their complexions
> were different. I am not ashamed to say, though I
> may expose myself to ridicule in saying so, that once
> I have witnessed the redemption of Israel, my people,
> I wish to assist in the redemption of the Africans.

Despite great difficulties and obstacles, the ten-year-old
state of Israel was going ahead with all possible speed
toward the social reconstruction and human rehabilitation
which was her raison d'être. Now, Golda declared, it was
time to reach out and share Israel's hard-earned experience
and her resources with other new states faced with similar
problems.

Her brand of diplomacy was something Ghana had never
seen before. At a conventional farewell cocktail party at a
hotel in Accra, Golda led her entourage into a spirited hora
in which they were joined by a handful of young Ghanaians
who had spent some time in kibbutzim. The waiters were
bewildered and a few Europeans looked shocked, but soon
the Ghanaian cabinet ministers and tribal chiefs caught the
rhythm and joined in.

One newspaper reported: "When almost everyone else
was ready to give up, the Foreign Minister, glistening with
perspiration, continued dancing with one of the hosts."

The Ghanaians reciprocated by striking up "high life,"
the most rhythmic of all the Gold Coast dances. No non-
African could hope to master the deceptively simple steps,
but Golda danced bravely with one of the ministers, winning
applause and an A for effort.

In Nigeria an official said to her: "Your Foreign Ministry
is mislabeled 'foreign.' To us it is a Friendly Ministry."

Golda had been told that what Africans most wanted to
learn was what Israel could best teach: how to do things
cooperatively, how to increase food production, how to irri-
gate eroded soil and make it fertile, how to combat malnu-

trition, trachoma, high infant mortality. The list of needs was endless.

On her return to Israel, Golda reported: "They all seem to think that Israel has an endless reserve of specialists. If there is any problem, the best solution is to ask for an Israeli expert and there you are! But," she added, "I hope we'll find it possible to spare quite a few good men and women to help those peoples solve some of their problems."

And so was born the highly successful Israel International Cooperation Program.

At the invitation of an African government, Israeli experts, usually a single expert but sometimes two or three, went to the country, rolled up their sleeves, and demonstrated by the example of their own labor how to do whatever was called for.

"I met a Kenyan," Golda said, "who exclaimed to me in amazement: 'For the first time I've seen a white man work with his hands.'"

Generally, the Israelis remained with the project for an initial two-year hitch, but often this was extended in order to make sure that the Africans they were training could take over and carry the program on effectively. Many Africans were invited to come to Israel for additional training in the kibbutzim, at the university and in hospitals, and in factories and mills. Then they would return home to use their know-how in their own villages.

In 1960 Golda made another African tour, this time to Ghana, Guinea, Sierre Leone, Togo, Dahomey, and Niger. Everywhere she was treated as an old friend, one who listened with understanding and sympathy and who could be relied upon to translate this understanding and sympathy into action.

She never tired of making the rounds of Israeli projects, both those still under way and those successfully completed.

"Imagine!" she reported to the Israeli cabinet. "Outside

Foreign Minister Golda Meir with a Tanganyikan participant
at an Afro-Asian seminar in Haifa, 1961
(Photo: Oskar Tauber, Haifa)

Abidjan, hundreds of girls from the villages who were at the level of witchcraft have been trained to do community work!"

At Haifa in 1961 Golda was hostess to a six-week Afro-Asian seminar on the role of women in a developing society, which was attended by delegates from twenty-three nations, the majority African. A letter from one of the delegations was among Golda's treasured souvenirs:

> We are now more aware of problems existing in our own countries. We have more courage to face the challenges and to realize that we women, as educators of the nation, should no longer expect to be spoon-fed or wait for manna to fall from heaven. Having been to Israel, to this land of promise, flowing with milk and honey, we are quite full of inspiration to return home and get down to the task of working out our future heritage.
>
> God bless Israel! Shalom! Shalom!

At one point the Arab states attacked Israel's International Cooperation Program in the United Nations, and Golda's reply was dipped in acid: "An especially pathetic warning was given by Arab speakers at the general debate to African states against Israel's alleged 'colonialism.'

"If an Israeli poultry expert is engaged by an African country, does that make the chickens 'colonialist' chickens? If Israel and an African country cooperate in shipping services, does that make the vessels 'imperialist' vessels? Are the many hundreds of trainees from African countries in Israel in agriculture, cooperatives, et cetera, training in colonialism? We know this is nonsense. The Arabs know it is nonsense, and, what is more important, the Africans themselves know it is nonsense."

She refused to play politics with the program. On one occasion when Ghana voted against Israel in the United

Nations Golda was asked by some members of the Israeli Government "to get even" by withholding aid.

Golda was furious. "What Israel is doing in Africa is more than 'policy.' It is a continuation of all the traditions of the Jewish people. Should Israel make the dispatch of doctors to fight malaria or trachoma contingent on the way an African state votes at the United Nations? Such a quid pro quo would be more than a political failure. It would be a failure of Israel's historic instincts. This Foreign Ministry will not take that path."

When the International Cooperation Program celebrated its tenth anniversary, a total of 2,582 Israeli experts had participated in the program: 916 in agriculture, 354 in youth organizations, 262 in medicine and health, 230 in education, 246 in technology, and 566 in other fields. The largest number of experts, 1,719, had gone to Africa; 350 had gone to the Mediterranean area, 258 to Latin America and the Caribbean, and 255 to Asia.

"How do you account for the success of your program, especially in Africa?" the American evangelist Billy Graham once asked Golda.

Golda smiled. "That's easy," she said. "We go there to teach, not to preach."

The success of the program in faraway places often made her think with deep yearning of how well it could work with the Arabs just across Israel's borders, given conditions of peace.

"Yes," she said, "Israel has sent thousands of men and women to other continents to bring to the people the results of our experience, to work with them as brothers, to help them in their development plans. It will be a great day when we don't have to travel thousands of miles and tens of thousands of miles, and the young Jew from this side of the Jordan on his farm will cross the Jordan, not with tanks, not with planes, but with tractors and with the hand of friendship as between farmer and farmer, as human being and human being. A dream? Maybe. I am sure it will come true."

In 1964 Golda Meir, like thousands of other Israelis, applied for old-age benefits under the National Insurance Law, which she had introduced during her term as Minister of Labor, stating that she was still "actively employed" and worked "sixteen hours a day, thirty days a month."

She was sixty-six years old and beginning to think of retirement.

CHAPTER 17

The Golda Era

IN THE OPINION of her colleagues what Golda needed was time out, not retirement, and her political secretary, Simcha Dinitz, suggested that she take a vacation.

"Why?" she asked. "Do you think I'm tired?"

"No," he said, "but I am."

"So *you* take a vacation," Golda retorted.

But she was weary, and her weariness was compounded by worry over the threat to Mapai's unity posed by Ben-Gurion's erratic behavior over the last few years. She had remained unswervingly loyal to him, but their friendship was being considerably strained by what she regarded as his encroachments on her office as Foreign Minister and by several sharp divisions of opinion with respect to policy. In 1963 Ben-Gurion had abruptly resigned, appointed Levi Eshkol to serve the remaining two years of his term as Prime Minister, retired to his kibbutz in the Negev, and then proceeded to criticize and bitterly attack his own appointee. As the 1965 elections approached, Ben-Gurion announced that he had decided to return to public life as head of a new political party called Rafi. At great personal cost, Golda broke with Ben-Gurion and threw her support to Eshkol, who asked her to remain as Foreign Minister at least until the elections were over.

When Eshkol won the election by a wide margin, Golda felt that she could safely resign, and early in 1966 she an-

The Prime Minister wheels her newest grandchild along a Jerusalem street.

nounced her retirement. She had served in all of Israel's cabinets since the first Knesset election in 1949, and at a farewell ceremony the ministers presented her with a metal relief map of the world, with every Israeli diplomatic mission marked by semiprecious stones from the Negev. She moved out of the official residence in Jerusalem into a modest house in Tel Aviv, which she shared with Menahem and his family. At last, she thought, she would have time to read, to vacation at Revivim, enjoying her grandchildren and the now green and flourishing kibbutz in the Negev, to rest and clear up the recurring circulatory ailment that plagued her.

But whether she was in or out of office, government decisions, as one of the current jokes in Israel put it, were still being cooked in Golda's kitchen. Her unrivaled prestige and moral authority were indispensable to her party, and within a few months of her resignation she was drafted to take over as Secretary-General of Mapai.

These were again critical times for Israel. The country was suffering a general economic slowdown, a recession, and a renewed crisis, which ultimately threatened war with the Arabs.

The crisis could be traced to the first Arab Summit Conference of January, 1964, convened by President Nasser to consider Syria's demand for aggressive action against Israel. In a repeat performance of 1956 a unified command was set up, and the Palestine Liberation Organization was established to recruit guerrillas for acts of terrorism against Israel across the Syrian and Jordanian borders. In September of the same year the conference voted a huge sum to stockpile arms in Syria, Lebanon, and Jordan.

By 1965 Al Fatah terrorists, based in Damascus, were making sabotage and murder raids into Israel, and after the military coup in Syria in 1966, artillery attacks were mounted from the Golan Heights against Israeli settlements in the valley below.

In May, 1966, the Syrian leader, Nureddin al-Attasi, announced: "We want a full-scale total war of liberation, not only to destroy the Zionist base in Palestine, but also to destroy the oil monopolies and imperialist and reactionary interests."

And, once again, as before the Sinai Campaign, Israel could not write off these threats as either bravado or empty rhetoric. The Soviet Union was pouring jet fighters and bombers, heavy and medium tanks, ground-to-air and ground-to-ground missiles, and naval equipment into the Arab states. Then, not content with providing arms for a third-round war against Israel, the Soviets sought to bring the simmering caldron of the Middle East to a boil by making an inflammatory and totally false accusation against Israel in the United Nations.

On October 14, 1966, the Soviet ambassador, Nikolai Federenko, charged: "There has been a partial mobilization of reserves in Israel. In addition there is information showing that an air attack is being prepared in Israel against neighboring Syrian territory in preparation for the intrusion of Israel forces deep in Syrian territory."

The United Nations Truce Supervision Organization investigated the Soviet charge and reported it to be completely without foundation.

This did not deter the Soviets from repeating the charge, but when the Soviet ambassador in Israel complained to Prime Minister Eshkol about "heavy troop concentrations in the north" and was invited to visit the area, he refused.

Golda Meir told reporters: "Friends, those of you who have been in Israel or have seen the map, know that our Syrian border is not so long that you can mass an army for attack and not see it. But the Soviet ambassador naturally wouldn't go because, God forbid, had he gone up, he would have found out that everything that comes out from the Kremlin in the press and the radio is lies, and he didn't want to have it proved to him. He knew, himself, that this was a lie. He knew there was no army massed on the Syrian border."

The only "concentrations" on the border were frightened children huddled in kibbutz shelters against artillery barrages from the Golan Heights. But the Soviet lie provided Nasser with "grounds" for moving his forces into the Sinai on May 14, 1967, in order to come to the "defense" of Syria. Then, on May 16, the Egyptian command ordered the United Nations Emergency Force, which was charged with supervising the cease-fire, to leave Sharm-el-Sheikh and the Sinai Peninsula, and the Secretary-General of the United Nations, U Thant, consented. On May 22 Nasser announced that he was reimposing the Gulf of 'Aqaba blockade against Israeli ships and cargoes.

"The Jews threaten war," Nasser said, "and we say, by all means, we are ready for war."

In the United States President Lyndon B. Johnson tried to get the other powers to join in upholding what they had "guaranteed" Israel—the right of free passage in exchange for her withdrawal after the Sinai Campaign. But Britain and France refused, since they wanted no part in the coming confrontation in the Middle East.

Prime Minister Eshkol delivered a message calling for deescalation of the forces massing on Israel's borders. The Egyptian reply came over Radio Cairo on May 25:

"The Arab people is firmly resolved to wipe Israel off the map and restore the honor of the Arabs of Palestine."

By June 4 Egypt had massed ninety thousand troops and nine hundred tanks on the Sinai border with an additional two hundred tanks concentrated for direct attack against Israel's southern port of Elath, and six hundred aircraft ready to strike at Israel's airfields and cities. Over 45,000 Syrian troops were poised on the Golan Heights, and Jordan had moved tanks and artillery to a sector where the distance across Israel's narrow waist to the Mediterranean was less than ten miles.

Although out of the Government, Golda Meir participated in the decisions Israel must make as to her capability and the nature of her response. Approximately 2.5 million Israelis must face 40 million Arabs. Defeat by the Arabs would not mean occupation by a victorious army but being wiped out in another holocaust.

"I understand the Arabs wanting to wipe us out," Golda said, "but do they really expect us to cooperate? We intend to remain alive. Our neighbors want to see us dead. This is not a question that leaves much room for compromise." And then, looking from Eshkol to Chief of Staff Itzhak Rabin, the indomitable sixty-nine-year-old grandmother added, "I don't see how war can be avoided. Nobody is going to help us. But I'm convinced that we'll win."

Israel struck first, as she must, to survive. She attacked on the morning of June 5, 1967, and in six incredible days, which electrified the world, Israel drove Egypt out of the Sinai and Gaza, occupied the Golan Heights and Jordan's West Bank, and reunified Jerusalem.

Again, Golda summed up the events in her own fashion: "On the morning of June 5, 1967, Levi Eshkol sent a message to King Hussein telling him: 'If you don't come into the war, nothing will happen to you.'

"That same morning, Hussein received another message. This one was from President Nasser, who, after the Egyptian Air Force had been practically wiped out, told Hussein: 'I have destroyed seventy-five percent of the Israeli Air Force. Come in!'

"At the same time, Nasser also sent a message to his friends in Syria, saying: 'Seventy-five percent of my Air Force has been destroyed. Stay out.'"

The Russians had also stayed out and did nothing to help their Arab protégés, mindful of the United States Sixth

Fleet on full war alert in the Mediterranean, ready to help
Israel if need be.

The United Nations called for a cease-fire and refused to
label Israel the aggressor in spite of the howling for punitive
action against her by the Arab and Soviet blocs.

But there was little jubilation in Israel—only a mass sigh
of relief that for the third time Israel had successfully defended her right to exist.

"We don't want wars even when we win," Golda said.
"The Israelis have no joy in killing, no joy in shooting,
no joy in winning wars. The Israeli soldiers were the sad-
dest victorious army in history."

Golda remained at the helm of the Mapai, and by January, 1968, she had achieved her objective, which was to
guide the party through the negotiations leading to a mer-
ger of Mapai, Achdut Haavoda, and Rifi into a unified Israel
Labor party. She remained as Secretary-General for the first
critical months, then announced her resignation in August,
1968.

This time, she said, she was *really* retiring, but, she
added: "I am not going into a political wilderness. I do
not intend to retire to a political convent."

Now she had time to read, to cook and bake; to visit
Menahem and his family at the University of Connecticut,
where he was teaching cello and his wife, Ayah, had a grant
in psychiatry. She saw more of her family in Revivim, and
there was, finally, time for visits with her old friends.

But only six months later, on February 29, 1969, Prime
Minister Levi Eshkol suffered a fatal heart attack, and
Golda Meir was summoned to meet the most extraordinary
challenge of her entire career.

Others were suggested to replace Eshkol. Men like Rabin
and Dayan, heroes of the Six Day War, as the fighting of
June, 1967, had been labeled, or Yigal Allon, the Deputy
Prime Minister. But the inner councils of the recently

merged Labor party decided that only Golda had the experience, authority, and prestige to form and hold together a cabinet that would be, as political observers remarked, "a wall-to-wall coalition government."

"But Golda's an old sick woman," some members of the party protested.

To which Golda retorted: "Being seventy is not a sin," and added, "It's not a joy, either."

Although Golda told intimates she was enjoying her retirement, such keen-eyed old friends as Regina felt that retirement was not a happy state for her.

"Golda's career was such a natural thing for her," Regina said. "When she said she was going to retire, she seemed to cave in all of a sudden. She just isn't built for retirement. When she was asked to become Prime Minister, it was like an injection of new life; she perked up, and the years fell away from her."

She had reached the summit of her career, yet she had not climbed toward it, rung by rung, following any blueprint.

"I can honestly say that never in my life have I planned what position I would like to have," she commented. "I planned to come to Palestine. I planned to go to a kibbutz. And I planned to be in the Labor movement. But what position I would occupy? Never."

On March 7, 1969, the Central Committee of the Labor party voted by a huge majority to appoint Golda Meir as Prime Minister, and on March 17 she presented her cabinet to the Knesset and received the largest vote of confidence of any government since Israel's independence.

Many Israelis within and without the Government assumed that Golda would be an interim Prime Minister, serving until the new elections were held seven months later, in October.

But Golda punctured this assumption at her first conference for the foreign press, shortly after taking office.

A reporter asked: "When your appointment was first broached, you said you'd be a stopgap. Do you expect to be a stopgap?"

Golda stared at him. "Did I say I was a stopgap?"

"You didn't, but others did."

"Well, then," Golda said, "they should be asked the question."

How would this seventy-year-old grandmother lead an all-male cabinet, people wondered, and Golda, well aware of the uniqueness of her position, quipped:

"When my colleagues, men, look at me now, a bit sad, and wonder what is going to happen to them after all, I say: 'Don't worry. We will see to it, we women, that you have the right to vote and equal pay for equal work. And once in a while, we will even elect a man as Prime Minister!' "

The Golda Era had begun.

The stamina of the "old sick woman" was formidable: She was present at every cabinet meeting, averaged three speeches a week throughout the country, visited the troops in the newly occupied territories, and taking advantage of a woman's prerogative, hugged several of the soldiers as she passed in review. As always, she was impatient of security restrictions, and whenever her car drove past soldiers hitchhiking home, she ground her teeth in annoyance because she was forbidden to give rides. Her personal bodyguard was a handsome, twenty-three-year-old Iraqi Jew, Mordechai Rahamim, the security agent who had defended an El Al airliner against an Arab guerrilla attack at the Zurich airport in February, 1969, and had become a national hero. He was certain to steal the show from Golda when they appeared in public together, but she did not in the least mind. On one of her visits to Revivim everybody raced for autographs—from Rahamim. The Prime Minister squinched her eyes shut and laughed.

As Premier, Golda ran her cabinet like a frontline officer, thumping the table for order and making blunt and rapid decisions. From the outset, Golda made clear to her cabinet what she considered was the responsibility of government:

"I think it is the duty of government to decide what it thinks is for the best, to the best of its knowledge and ability to analyze a problem, and when convinced that it has come to the right conclusion, it must bear the consequences. We will not make a poll of what the people think and then decide accordingly, because then you don't need a government at all. It would be enough to have a bureau of statistics or have public relations make a poll, and then the decision is automatic. I don't believe in that kind of government.

"In a parliamentary regime our government has to have the courage to make decisions on the merits of the case, and only on the merits, and face parliament. And either parliament supports the government, or it can go home."

She listened to everyone but interrupted if they rambled. She had an open mind, but arguing with her was like arguing before a judge; when she made a decision, it was made. Her handling of dissent within the cabinet was firm but, characteristically, with as light a touch as possible.

An angry minister, miffed because she would not go along with a plan of his, said accusingly, "It's only you who don't agree with me."

Golda shrugged: "All right, then, dissolve me, but don't dissolve the cabinet."

At times rivalries among the younger members of her cabinet threatened to get out of hand as in one instance between her Minister of Defense, Moshe Dayan, and Deputy Prime Minister Yigal Allon.

Golda shook her head at both of them. "I'd like to see the war with the Arabs finished," she sighed, "before the war of the Jews begins."

It was a foregone conclusion that the "interim" Prime Minister would be elected to a full term in office in October, 1969. Sixteen parties vied for the 120 seats in the Knesset, and the Labor alignment, led by Golda Meir, won half the seats in a victory that everyone interpreted as a personal triumph for her.

"This is an awful job," she said candidly. "It's not the work. God knows, before I came to this office, I was not given an opportunity to be spoiled by leisure. I only dreamt about it. But the responsibility. It's an awful strain. I imagine it would be at any time, but at this time . . ."

CHAPTER 18

"Israel Is So Big in Spite of Its Smallness!"

FOREMOST AMONG GOLDA's priorities was to strive for a just and lasting peace for Israel within the framework of the United Nations resolution of November 22, 1967, calling for "withdrawal of Israeli armed forces from territories occupied during the recent conflict"; "termination of all claims or states of belligerency"; recognition of the sovereignty of every state in the area and "their right to live in peace within secure and recognized borders free from threats or acts of force; freedom of navigation through international waterways; and a just settlement of the refugee problem."

In March, 1968, Dr. Gunnar V. Jarring of Sweden, who had been appointed by the Secretary-General of the United Nations to promote agreement between the parties of the Middle East, asked Egypt, Jordan, and Israel to send representatives to a meeting under his auspices. Syria had refused to accept the United Nations resolution and insisted on remaining outside its framework, but Egypt and Jordan had accepted it. But when Israel announced her willingness to meet Arab representatives at any time and any place to hold face-to-face talks, Egypt demanded as a precondition that Israel must first withdraw from "all" territories taken in the Six Day War and return to the boundaries exactly as they existed on June 4, 1967.

This, Israel would not do.

"Nobody has yet proved to us," Golda said, "why it is so outlandish for us to expect that after three wars, we should have a signed peace agreement, something that usually takes place between the parties in any war. The only peculiar aspect of the situation is that the party that is asking for this contractual agreement is not the party that lost the war but the party that won the war. With Arabs who want to live in peace with the state of Israel, we shall negotiate everything. We have decided that this is enough! We have enough victories!"

As a way out of the impasse, Charles de Gaulle suggested that the United States, Britain, the Soviet Union, and France enter into four-power talks in order to arrive at a "settlement" of the Middle East problems.

"I am especially impressed when we are told that a partner to the search for peace in the area is the Soviet Union, since its contribution to peace in the Middle East has been, thus far, outstanding," Golda commented, and added that France, too, having placed under embargo the planes that Israel had ordered and paid for, would scarcely be prejudiced in Israel's favor.

In a full-scale address before the Knesset the Prime Minister made clear to the Big Four that not only must Israel be permitted, like any other sovereign state, to determine its own fate but that intercession by the big powers and an attempt to impose a settlement without direct negotiation with the Arab states leading to a signed peace agreement would not further the cause of peace but obstruct it.

Yet, increasingly, pressure was put upon Golda to reverse her "intransigent" position.

"We get tired sometimes of all the compliments we receive," Golda replied. "About how we are so rational, so intelligent, and because the Arabs are emotional and irrational, it is we who have to be the reasonable ones. What is really being said to us? It is: 'You have to give in.'"

As the pressure on Israel to yield mounted, world opinion, which had cheered her victory in the Six Day War, now, perversely, went against her. Was it, Golda wondered, because Israel was no longer weak, an object of pity, that she had come into disfavor? Eschewing the language of diplomacy which, in her opinion, was often just so much double-talk, Golda stated and restated Israel's case at press conferences and in radio and television interviews, underscoring the irony of the situation:

"A wonderful people these Israelis!" she exclaimed. "They win wars every ten years, whatever the odds. Fantastic! Now that they have won this round, let them go back where they came from, so that Syrian gunners on the Golan Heights can shoot into the kibbutzim, so that Jordanian legionnaires on the towers of the Old City in Jerusalem can again shell at will, so that the Gaza Strip can again be a nest for terrorism, so that the Sinai Desert can again become the staging ground for Nasser's divisions.

"We're told over and over again that Nasser is frustrated. Frustrated as a result of what?" she demanded. "Because three times he tried to destroy us and didn't succeed, poor man? So I should have sympathy for him? And we mustn't ask him to sit down with us and negotiate a peace agreement?"

Israel would not again accept what Golda described as another peace "gimmick." Everything had been tried—United Nations police forces, "guarantees" by the big powers—and none of them had secured and maintained peace in the area. This time Israel would stand fast on the cease-fire lines, for she would not withdraw until secure, recognized, and agreed borders were worked out between the Arabs and Israelis in a signed peace agreement.

The Arab policy toward Israel remained adamantly grounded on three points: no recognition, no negotiation, no peace.

And looming ever larger in aid of this policy were the Palestinian commando organizations which, after the "humiliation" of the Six Day War, began to burgeon. The Palestine Liberation Organization, founded in 1964 under the aegis of the fourteen-nation Arab League, came under Al Fatah's control in 1969, led by Yasir Arafat. The ten member organizations were connected in a loose chain of command, with frequent shifts in alignment and with different areas of concentration: Al Fatah mounted military forays into Israel and Israeli-occupied areas; the Popular Front for the Liberation of Palestine specialized in acts of terrorism outside the Middle East, such as hijackings and bombings; the Popular Struggle Front engaged in general terrorist activities; and so on.

These fedayeen were enraged at their governments' surrender to Israel. They declared that they represented the true will of the people and that the governments were so corrupt that they would eventually collapse and give way to an all-Arab people's government.

Despite the fedayeens' opposition to existing Arab regimes, the evidence of wide popular support for them led Nasser to give them his official blessing in a Radio Cairo message in January, 1969:

"Al Fatah fulfills a vital task in sapping the enemy's strength and drawing his blood. . . . The U.A.R. appreciates the attitude taken by the Palestinian organizations in rejecting the Security Council resolution of November, 1967. . . ."

King Hussein of Jordan, feeling himself threatened by the fedayeens' rising power, threw his hat into the ring by declaring, "We are *all* fedayeen!"

But to recruit new members and acquire guns, rockets, mortars, vehicles, and uniforms required more than blessings or pats on the back. King Faisal of oil-rich Saudi Arabia, for one example, began to contribute about $100,000

Golda delivering a eulogy at the grave of an eighteen-year-old boy killed by Katyusha rocket while asleep at his home in Kiryat Shemona

a month to Al Fatah, and other Arab governments also lent their aid, so that the Palestine Liberation Organization received and divided some $2 million a year.

Among the exploits of these "heroes" and "sacrificers" was the time-bombing of a Swissair plane in March, 1970, in which forty-seven Israelis lost their lives, as did many non-Jewish passengers. As the flag-draped coffins were lined up in Jerusalem's Har Hamenuhot cemetery, a weeping Prime Minister, her face contorted in pain and anguish, delivered the eulogy over the victims of "this murder in the skies of Switzerland."

She concluded: "The heart burns with grief and rage. Let

us turn the sorrow and rage into a mighty force—real and moral—in the struggle against violence and murder. Let our anguish cry out to the world and our rage be a lever for action to eliminate the possibility of acts of murderers and those who shelter them, thereby making themselves immediate accomplices to the crime."

A few months later, in May, 1970, another band of "heroes," using Lebanon as their base, shot Russian-made Katyusha rockets at the town of Kiryat Shemona, in the Upper Galilee, one night killing an eighteen-year-old boy who was asleep in his bed and the next night killing a father and daughter.

Again the Prime Minister was on hand to attend the funeral. "These borders which were quiet for many years," she said, "have recently turned into the most turbulent. They know as we do that so long as they did not come across the border to sow death in our midst and did not fire rockets, we returned the peace faithfully. . . . We desire quiet on the borders on one condition: that there be quiet on *both* sides of the border."

The same day, Israel's Foreign Minister, Abba Eban, appealed to the Palestinians over Arab television and radio stations to take the alternative road to violence and cooperate for peace:

". . . make your voice heard in behalf of Israel-Arab negotiations which would promote peace and would solve once and for all the dispute that brought upon all of us—but especially upon you—torment and frustration, grief and untold suffering."

The fedayeen answer came a few days later: A rocket was lobbed at a crowded school bus, killing eleven children and wounding many others.

Still another reply came in the form of an outburst of Syrian artillery against Nahal Geshur, one of the farm settlements established by young soldier-farmers in the Israeli-occupied Golan Heights. Weeping Israeli girl soldiers in uniform attended the funeral of their comrade, an eighteen-year-old girl killed in the barrage, which also wounded four girls and two young men. The young settlers announced that they would stay on in their outpost despite the threat of more shellings from the Syrian border only a few miles away.

Golda's Government decided to retaliate for these acts of terrorism "sevenfold" and sent Israeli units across the borders to destroy guerrilla bases, arms caches, and installations. After each of these reprisals by the Israelis, the Arab bloc arose in the United Nations, demanding that the "aggressors" be censured, and Arab propagandists, well supplied with funds, bombarded the media and American campuses seeking—and often obtaining—support for their War of Liberation.

"If there is anything that horrified me in the past year," Golda told reporters, "it is not that people criticize us. That is absolutely legitimate, even if we don't like it and would rather hear praise. What does horrify me is that murderers are played up as heroes and that suddenly the Arabs are waging a 'war of liberation'—which is fought by hiding a bomb in a student cafeteria." Or setting off an explosion in a parked car in a crowded street in Tel Aviv. Or throwing a grenade into a Jerusalem supermarket when it was jammed with housewives shopping in advance of the Sabbath.

Yet the Israelis' morale remained high. The people in the cities calmly went about their business, and the settlers in the villages and kibbutzim in the Jordan and Beisan valleys, which were shelled from across the Jordan River by day and by night, remained steadfast.

"Their children have actually been living in bomb shelters for a year and a half now," Golda observed, "but not a single settler has budged."

In contrast, she described the Jordanian side with its villages abandoned by sixty thousand farmers who had fled
from the depredations of their own kinsmen.

With respect to the Arabs who remained in Israeli-occupied Gaza and Jordan's West Bank, she pursued this policy:
"We are responsible for the welfare of its people. We have
to do everything we possibly can, whether it is in economic
development, certainly in employment, in social services, in
every way, to see that the people are taken care of."

But she refused to consider negotiating with Al Fatah or
any of the other terrorist groups. As far as she was concerned, they were murderers, not liberators.

"Yasir Arafat now says he doesn't want to liberate the
West Bank. He wants to liberate the entire Palestinian area,"
Golda said, her eyebrows raised. "And this means he wants
to liberate our area. He says he's prepared to negotiate with
Arab countries and that they should take back the Jews who
came from them. Iraqi Jews should go back to Iraq, and
maybe the first thing they should do is to go to the market-
place and see where they hang Jews and other people. Libyan Jews should go back to the caves in Libya where they
came from. And," she concluded, smiling broadly, "I should
go back to Milwaukee!"

To the often repeated Arab charge that Israelis were
westernized intruders bent upon aggrandizement in a Mus-
lim Middle East, Golda replied:

"If this means that we have brought in a modern phase
of thinking, we have. I came to Israel in 1921. One of the
first sights that shocked me was an Arab ploughing with a
very primitive plough, which was really just a piece of wood
with some nails below. Pulling the plough were an ox and
a woman. Now if it means that we have destroyed this romantic picture by bringing in tractors and combines and
threshing machines, this is true, we have. . . . As for aggrandizement, nobody can honestly claim that the war of

1967 broke out because Israel wanted more territory. All that we did in 1967, fortunately for ourselves, was to carry the war on to enemy soil instead of fighting on Israeli soil. Anybody who is attacked tries to do that."

The Prime Minister felt that the accusation of aggrandizement should be leveled instead at the Soviet Union, which had already eroded the independence and sovereignty of Egypt. Thousands of Soviet technicians, pilots, and advisers were now based in Egypt, making a mockery of the so-called independence of the Arab world.

Another of the insistent Arab demands was that Israel permit the one and a half million people who called themselves refugees to choose whether they wished to enter Israel.

"I used to say to all the friends who used to suggest this, that they should leave us at least one privilege," Golda said. "If the state of Israel and the people of Israel should decide to commit suicide, give them the right of free choice to decide by what means to do it.

"The fact is that we have taken back thousands of refugees under family reunion plans: we have never said: 'Not a single refugee.' But free choice to all would mean that Al Fatah would have a free choice of whichever they found more convenient: to shell us from the other side of the border or to destroy us inside our own territory, and this we are not prepared to allow them to do."

The most troublesome front was the Suez Canal. Nasser had again grandiosely announced that his plans for a fourth round with Israel were formulated and under way. First, however, his army must be rebuilt, and the Russians, despite the enormous losses they had taken in arms destroyed or captured by the Israelis in the Six Day War, were pouring in more guns, tanks, planes, and Russian personnel, bringing Nasser's forces up to and even beyond previous levels. The next step was to wage a war of attrition—of

continuous harassment—to weaken and demoralize the Israelis. After that would come what Golda described as "the
big act."

In the month of August, 1968, alone, over five hundred
violations of the cease-fire had been committed by Egypt
in the Suez Canal area, including opening fire, shellings,
sabotage, and laying mines.

The Israelis refused to sit on their side of the canal and
take all this flak. They countered with barrages across the
canal and then by air strikes deep into Egypt, at the bases
from which commando units were laying mines and launch-
ing attacks against Israeli positions.

"The fact is," Golda reported to her people, "that the war
of attrition's been turned right around. It's working the
other way."

That was the Prime Minister talking. Golda Meir, mother
and grandmother, instructed her political secretary, Simcha
Dinitz: "Phone me as soon as the boys come home."

Dinitz would be called by the army, and then he would
phone Golda at two or three or four in the morning. She always answered at the first ring. At such times she never
slept.

To risk the life of even one Israeli was the most painful
of necessities. Yet she knew that these reprisals were the
only way of driving home to the Egyptian leaders and the
other Arab states the hard fact that their aggressive acts
would elicit punitive reprisals.

"We're not bombing the interior to force Nasser to make
peace," she explained. "We go into the interior to make it
well known to the people of Egypt that there must be quiet
on both sides of the canal. Nasser can't lie anymore to his
people when they hear our planes right near Cairo. They
know then that they can't have it both ways."

Yet the Prime Minister and her Government refused to
concentrate exclusively on military problems or even on

political or international problems. Israel's leaders, unlike
the leaders of the Arab countries who invested all their energy and resources into the military struggle against Israel,
insisted that the country continue to develop and rebuild.

"Take, for example, our educational program," Golda
said proudly. "We voted in a law this year to raise the age
for free compulsory education from fourteen to fifteen. In
two years that will go up to sixteen. You might ask why, in
this year when we are bearing such a heavy burden of defense, we are so concerned with education. We know that
it's impossible to do otherwise: Education must continue and
be extended even further than before. Equally, we must ac-
celerate agricultural, industrial, and scientific development.

"All this must go together because we can't preoccupy ourselves solely with our defense, although, most certainly, if
we allow ourselves to weaken, everything else would be
jeopardized."

These were the twin problems of Israel—security and in-
ternal development—and the Prime Minister felt that she
had only one friend in all the world who had never failed to
listen to her needs and to help, the United States. When
President Richard Nixon invited Israel's Premier to visit
him late in September, 1969, Golda was extremely glad of
the opportunity for a personal meeting and discussions.

But, for once, even she was rattled. "I want to admit,"
she declared, "that when I think of coming to the United
States at the invitation of the President, I am scared.
Scared because of the responsibility that rests on my
shoulders to represent Israel. It isn't simple. Israel is so
big in spite of its smallness—one must be conscious of one's
inability to represent it properly. But I have that—the
consciousness of the inability."

As it turned out, Golda did not have a thing to worry
about.

CHAPTER 19

What Can You Do?
She's Irresistible!

THE CLIMATE OF public opinion in the United States was once again more sympathetic toward Israel, as Americans became revolted by Arab excesses: hijackings, public hangings, and renewed cries for a "Holy War."

On August 29, 1969, Arab commandos hijacked a Trans World Airlines aircraft to Syria. "At a shocking risk to the lives of the passengers and crew and by a coarse infringement of all the principles of free international aviation," Golda said in a Kol Israel broadcast, "a gang of criminals [fedayeen] gained control of a civilian aircraft bearing the flag of the United States and forced the pilot to land in Damascus."

While the other passengers were released, the Syrians held two Israeli civilians: Dr. Shlomo Samueloff, a well-known physiologist, and Mr. Salah Muallem, who was in the tourist business. After three months of intensive negotiations involving the United Nations, the International Red Cross, and the United States State Department, the Syrians finally released the two Israelis in an exchange for Arab prisoners, chiefly soldiers, at a ratio of nearly 20 to 1.

In Iraq, as a reprisal for the Six Day War, fifty-three persons, including eleven Jews, were executed in a mass hanging in the Baghdad public square on trumped-up charges of espionage while the people turned the sickening spectacle into a carnival. Seven other Jews were tortured to death, and dozens of others were jailed and held incommunicado from their families and the rest of the outside world.

In Syria, too, a Jewish community of some four thousand were being persecuted, placed under house arrest, or thrown into jails. The lives of the fifteen hundred Jews in Egypt were in constant danger, and many were jailed without specific charges against them except the crime of being Jewish.

To top it all off, Nasser was again making announcements about waging a "Holy War" against Israel and driving the Israelis into the sea.

A few weeks before Golda's visit scheduled for September 25 and 26, 1969, she took time out from her normal duties to prepare a "shopping list" to take with her to the White House. One of her key consultants was her Minister of Defense, Moshe Dayan, for heading the list were items needed for the defense of Israel: additional Phantom jets after the fifty aircraft already on order were delivered, Hawk ground-to-air missiles, Skyhawk attack bombers, and still other pieces of military hardware.

"Yes," Golda admitted, "our military people have quite a shopping list that they would like to have filled, and I hope it will be. But we would be happy to throw all the hardware into the sea, or, at any rate, to stop spending one single penny on additional hardware because there are many other things that we enjoy spending money on more than on tanks or planes. Yet there must be a fair balance of power between us and all the others in our neighborhood until the day when there will be a real peace."

Despite a leaping growth rate in Israel, it could not keep pace with the vast sums that must be spent on armaments. As a result, Israel's economic reserves had declined sharply, and Golda would be seeking long-term, low-interest loans to bolster the economy.

On the diplomatic front Golda hoped to convince President Nixon that the cause of peace in the Middle East would best be served by stopping the big-power talks which looked toward an "imposed" settlement. How could anything acceptable to Israel come from a Soviet "peace" effort?

Upon arrival with her entourage at Philadelphia and welcoming speeches from the governor of the state and mayor of the city, Golda proceeded by motorcade to Independence Square, where twenty thousand people had waited for hours for a good look at her. Young people were everywhere carrying banners which said, "We dig you, Golda!" And Golda, smiling and waving, "dug" them right back.

"Have you ever seen anything like this?" Golda exclaimed over and over again.

But as a reporter on the scene remarked: "She could have read the telephone book to them, and they would have cheered. She has somehow found the bridge of love over the generation gap."

At 10:30 the following morning, September 25, Golda arrived at the White House by helicopter, then by limousine for the two-minute ride to the ceremonial area. President Nixon helped her out of the car, and the First Lady handed her a bouquet of roses. Hundreds of dignitaries, diplomats, and friends of Israel were gathered on the lawn, where a red carpet led to a raised platform. The President and the Prime Minister mounted it and stood at attention as the ceremony began with a nineteen-gun salute. The day was overcast, but as the Marine Band finished playing "The Star-Spangled Banner" and started to play "Hatikvah," the Israeli national anthem, the sun broke through the clouds.

President Nixon made a brief welcoming address which, significantly, stressed the United States' stake in peace in the Middle East and referred to Golda as "one of the world's leading women."

When it was Golda's turn to speak, she pulled a piece of paper from the large black pocketbook she always carried and read a short speech. The history of Israel, she said, could not be written without devoting a special chapter to the help America and its people had given. This was her only prepared text; for her other appearances, she would rely, as usual, on her own spontaneous, freewheeling style.

She met alone with the President for a little over an hour and a half, and there was no formal communiqué issued. Recognizing that it was up to the President to take the initiative in spelling out what they had talked about, Golda refused to be baited by the waiting press into saying more than she should.

Yes, she had a very friendly, good meeting with the President, and she was delighted with him. Yes, they had discussed Israel's long-range military and economic needs and had reviewed many problems of the Middle East in general.

"We enjoy the support of the United States," she continued, "and our aims are identical, although there are differences of opinion." She went on to praise the President for listening so intently and for his understanding of the Middle East situation. "He acted as if he had nothing to do except to listen to the troubles and problems of this little state!"

At another briefing session for the Israeli press, held in Hebrew, Golda was pressed very hard to tell more. She rebuked the reporters: "If I told you all about my talk with the President, you should be the first to let me have it over the head."

In Israel people were avidly reading every word in the press about "our Golda," and the Jerusalem Post, the English-language newspaper, proudly and affectionately described her visit to the Tomb of the Unknown Soldier at Arlington National Cemetery following her talk with the President:

It was a wonderfully paced, deeply moving ceremony carried out with uniformed pomp. Mrs. Meir wore a

simple, short-sleeved blue linen frock and had the inevitable black bag and gloves. A nineteen-gun salute
preceded the arrival of her limousine. Walking in
step with the medal-bedecked Adjutant General of
the United States Army, she proceeded at the head of
her entourage past an all-Service color guard. Then,
as everyone snapped to attention, a band played
"Hatikvah" in march-step speed followed by "The Star-
Spangled Banner."

The column set off again, with three high-stepping
color bearers carrying the Israeli flag at the head. At
the foot of each additional flight of stairs they waited
for Mrs. Meir to catch up. A little out of breath, she
placed an enormous wreath of giant blue-white chry-
santhemums on the marble tomb. There was a ruffle
of drums and taps played in a clear silver tone. For a
while, she was Prime Minister Meir, Head of Government of a foreign power.

That evening, President and Mrs. Nixon honored Golda
at a White House state dinner for 120 guests. In proposing a
toast to the Prime Minister, the President remarked that
it was the first time in his administration he had had the
honor to receive a head of government who was also a
woman.

"The people of Israel," he said, "have earned peace, not
the fragile peace that comes with the kind of document that
neither party has an interest in keeping but the kind of
peace that will last. We hope that as a result of our meeting
we will have taken a significant step forward toward that
peace which can mean so much to the people of Israel, to
the people of the Middle East, and also to the people of the
world."

Golda replied to the toast in a moving recital of Israel's
suffering in the past, her turbulent present, and the hope
for peace in the future.

"We are a people," she said, "who for two thousand years believed in the impossible. And here we are, a sovereign state, accepted in the family of nations, with many problems, many troubles, but here we are. There is idealism in this world. There is human brotherhood in this world. There is a great and powerful country, the United States, that feels that the existence of Israel is important to it because it is important that we all live and all exist no matter how small and how troubled we are.

"Mr. President, thank you, not only for your hospitality, not only for this great day and every moment that I had this day, but thank you for enabling me to go home and tell my people that we have a friend, a great friend and a dear friend. It will help. It will help us overcome many difficulties."

After dinner, which ended with a dessert called Revivim, the guests were entertained by two great American-Jewish musicians, Isaac Stern and Leonard Bernstein. While playing Ernest Bloch's "Jewish Melodies," Stern wept, and nearly everyone else in the room had tears in his eyes, not excepting the Prime Minister, for whom a most exceptional day was drawing to a close.

Next morning, Golda took her shopping list to Secretary of Defense Melvin Laird and held a closed meeting with him. Then she was off to a National Press Club luncheon where she utterly charmed the usually blasé newsmen with her plain speaking and wit.

Occasionally, she turned to her ambassador to Washington, General Itzhak Rabin, to give her an English equivalent for a Hebrew word, and everyone laughed at this former American schoolteacher who was at a loss for an English word.

"I guess," Golda smiled, "that fifty years away from America has done something to my English. But not to my arithmetic. At that I'm still good!"

Some of the questions would have trapped someone less adroit than Golda: "Would Israel employ nuclear weapons if her survival was in jeopardy?"

Golda fielded it with her usual aplomb: "It's such an iffy question, if we had the bomb, if we were in jeopardy, that I really don't know what to say. But," she added with a grin, "we haven't done so badly with conventional weapons."

She was asked what price Israel was willing to pay for peace.

"Our people have already paid for peace with the blood of their sons, and peace must be the real thing this time," she said. "Israel will draw no maps; everything will be put on the table—everything without preconditions. We are confident that we can get up from the table with a peace agreement fair to all."

The club's president thanked her and hoped that she would feel free to address the club again.

"Your grandson Gideon Meir says you make the best gefilte fish in Israel," he said. "Will you reveal your recipe to us?"

Golda laughed. "Gideon is hardly unprejudiced," she said. "I won't give you the recipe. I'll do better than that. When I come here again, I promise to arrive three days in advance and make gefilte fish for your luncheon."

Before leaving Washington, Golda had another private talk with the President, and afterward they appeared informally together before newsmen and photographers at the White House.

One of the pictures shows the President cracking up with laughter at one of Golda's rejoinders.

As a compliment to her effectiveness as Israel's spokesman, the President said, "The Prime Minister would make a great pinch hitter for the Senators."

Golda shot back, "I think I'm somewhat too old for that!"

The Prime Minister of Israel and the President of the United States share a joke.

No immediate announcement of additional American military and economic aid was made, but the President stated that they had arrived at a better understanding of how both countries should move from here on out.

Now that her business in Washington was concluded, Golda visited New York and Los Angeles, where she seized the opportunity to tell her audiences at dinners, meetings, and receptions and in magazine, radio, and television interviews about Israel's aspirations and needs and, above all, her desire for peace:

"We want peace, and we know that the masses of Arabs want it, too. I am convinced and honestly and sincerely believe that my grandchildren will live in an area of peace in the Middle East because there are other grandmothers in Egypt and Syria and Jordan that have grandchildren, and they also want them to live; and this desire is stronger than the fanatic desire of the leaders of the Arab people to kill others."

She had especially requested the opportunity of meeting with American-Jewish youth, and the mass rally at the Felt Forum in New York was unquestionably the high point of her visit. As she walked onstage, 3,600 young people gave her an eight-minute ovation, cheering and shouting, "Shalom, Golda!" Then they settled down to listen, giving her their total, rapt attention.

Her message was frankly one of Aliyah—Come to us! She described their counterparts, the young people of Israel:

"This is a wonderful generation—straight, fearless, beautiful, capable—there isn't a thing they can't do. And they want to study and they want to build and they want to create, and if they have to defend, they do it and know how. And they want more of you. They want to be many, and there is room in the country. And there are challenges in Israel now to every single one of you. There is something to do with one's life. There is hardship, there is difficulty, yes, and danger, but all this is worthwhile, there is a purpose. . . . Youth in Israel carry an immense burden on their shoulders, but they are free, and they are fighting and living and dying in order to assure a free and dignified future for the Jewish people.

"So many young volunteers came to Israel at the outbreak of the '67 war," she said, "to fight and die with us. Why can't young people come to live and build with us?"

Before leaving the country, Golda had promised herself the nostalgic pleasure of visiting Milwaukee and the public school she had entered in 1906, the year of her arrival in America. Then the children had all been white, of immigrant stock or, like Golda, immigrants themselves. Now all the children were black. As Golda entered the building, two little girls, dressed in Israel's colors, blue and white, and wearing white headbands with the Magen David (Star of David) on them, greeted her and gave her a large white paper carnation to wear.

"Shalom!" they said shyly.

Golda beamed, returned their greeting, then swooped them up to her bosom and kissed their shining black faces.

The corridors of the school were hung with the children's drawings of highlights of her life and the history of Israel; they sang for her in English and Hebrew and presented her with a scrapbook of letters and drawings.

The principal of the school read Golda's report-card marks aloud—nearly all the marks were A's—as well as various comments teachers had made on her behavior. One of the teachers had written about Golda: "Quite talkative."

Golda laughed. "No change," she whispered to the principal.

She held a final press conference before boarding an El Al airliner for home. On two of the three points that she had discussed with the President—arms and borders—Golda said she had received reassuring answers. While no specific numbers of aircraft were mentioned, "continued military assistance" when necessary would be extended to Israel.

On borders, Golda told the press: "The United States is not asking us to withdraw a single inch without peace. This is a great and wonderful thing. It's basic. It's a fact. Not only is there no pressure to withdraw, but we found absolute understanding."

The third point, advancing long-term, low-interest credit to Israel, was not actually within the power of the President to decide, since he did not hold the purse strings, but the outlook for a congressional appropriation was hopeful.

Summing up her visit, Golda said, "I am leaving with a much lighter heart than when I came."

The prospects for peace between Israel and her Arab neighbors remained remote, however. Then, in July, 1970, a breakthrough occurred when the United States took the initiative of proposing a cease-fire along the Suez Canal and the start of direct negotiations through Dr. Jarring to reach a peace settlement. On August 7, 1970, both Israel and Egypt accepted the cease-fire and began talks with Dr. Jarring at the United Nations headquarters in New York.

Almost at once, though, Egypt began to build a Soviet-supplied missile-defense system near the Suez Canal in violation of the agreement. Israel countered by refusing to participate further in the discussions until the Egyptian missile build-up was dismantled, and a deadlock resulted that lasted until December 28 when Golda and her cabinet decided to resume the discussions. What motivated the decision was the additional military aid provided by the United States which restored the military balance between Egypt and Israel.

In January, 1971, Dr. Jarring went to Jerusalem to call upon Golda. She told him that she saw little point in pursuing the talks energetically unless Egypt clearly stated that her purpose was "to make peace with Israel." She stressed the last two words because anything less specific would mean that Egypt still refused to recognize Israel's rights as a sovereign state.

On February 15, 1971, Egypt's new president, Anwar el-Sadat, who had been elected to office after Nasser's death, declared that his country was ready to reach a peace agreement with Israel but only on condition that Israel make a total withdrawal from all Arab areas occupied in the 1967 war. He had previously extended the February 7 date for the expiration of the Suez Canal cease-fire until

March 7, pending signs of progress in the Jarring talks, and now, he said, it was Israel's turn to make the next move.

Moments after Cairo formally terminated the cease-fire on March 7, Golda's Government made public Israel's proposals for "detailed and concrete" negotiations with the United Arab Republic. The essence of Israel's position was stated in the last paragraph: "Now that the U.A.R. has, through Ambassador Jarring, expressed its willingness to enter into a peace agreement with Israel and both parties have presented their basic positions, they should now pursue their negotiations in a detailed and concrete manner without prior conditions so as to cover all the points listed in their respective documents with a view to concluding a peace agreement."

The document reflected Golda Meir's conviction that only in negotiations could anything be resolved; Egypt was not expected to accept Israeli positions in advance of talks, and neither should Egypt place preconditions on Israel. The Israeli document did bluntly state, however, that "Israel will not withdraw to the pre–June 5, 1967, lines." Foreign officials, including those at the United States State Department who supported Israel's refusal to promise a total withdrawal, thought that this sentence would probably stall the peace talks again, but Golda believed in plain speaking: While Egypt continued to insist on Israel's total withdrawal instead of withdrawal to secure, agreed-upon borders, the talks would be only a diplomatic exercise.

How long the proposals and counterproposals would continue between Egypt and Israel and to what effect neither she nor anyone could accurately guess. There had been no shots fired between the two countries for seven months, however, and how could she count this other than a blessing? Also, for the first time after three wars, the Arabs were no longer speaking of pushing the Israelis into the sea but of making peace with them through a formal agreement.

So much had been gained, but so much remained in question! Golda felt she was duty bound to examine carefully every prospect, no matter how slim, that would lead to peace. What, after all, did the people of Israel and the people of the Middle East and the people of the world want and need more? Someday, she was sure, people would wonder, What could it mean that people went out and killed each other? She had no doubt whatever that one day there would be a world without wars. So much human decency existed among all people, in every field, in every area, in every walk of life. There was so much wealth and knowledge and progress in the world. An Israel at peace and a world at peace must come. But would she still be around to see it? She hoped so.

Epilogue

Open End

ON MAY 23, 1971, Prime Minister Golda Meir looked back to that day, a half century before, when she had boarded the S.S. *Pocahontas* and set sail for Palestine, aspiring to be one of the generation that dared to dream of a Jewish state and of attaining it.

Outside the windows of her Jerusalem office in the new government complex, she could see the horseshoe-shaped ridge of Givat Ram and the modern, templelike Knesset building at one end of it. On the opposite end of the horseshoe was Hebrew University with the great National Library. Facing the open end of the horseshoe were the cool, green-blue marble walls of the Israel Museum with its sculpture gardens and the Shrine of the Book, the home of the Dead Sea Scrolls.

Here was tangible evidence that Israel was a sovereign state, a free and independent nation. Yet how had it appeared that day of her arrival, fifty years before? The playwright and novelist Israel Zangwill had described it: "The land was waiting for the people and the people were waiting for the land."

This state of Israel had been created out of the sands of the Negev and the rocks of the Galilee. The children of Israel had been raised to conquer the desert and the rock. The desert had given way to cotton and wheat; forests and vineyards now covered the barren hills. During the Mandate they had gone out into the sea to meet the "illegal" boats

190

Golda reflects on a lifetime that took her from a desk in a Milwaukee schoolroom to the office of Prime Minister of Israel.

and carried the refugees from Hitler's horror to shore on their backs. They had taught the Yemenite and Iraqi and Syrian Jews the skills they needed to regain their human dignity and contribute to the development of the country.

The state of Israel was no transient thing, no foreign growth in the region, and its children could never be uprooted from their land, no matter how long and how loudly the Arabs contested their right to live there.

"I suppose it's taken us four thousand years to learn that Moses moved us into the wrong neighborhood!" Golda remarked to a group of young people, then joined in their laughter.

Uproot these young people? Never!

Their fathers had fought for the land in 1948, their older brothers had fought in 1956 and 1967, and now they, like her own granddaughter, just turning eighteen, were going into the army.

And it was this continuing, constant necessity to defend the land, forcing the children of Israel to learn to shoot and kill, that she would never forgive the Arabs for. Why? Why did the Arabs do this? But as long as they did, Israelis would have to be able to defend themselves.

Meanwhile, the fields of the country remained green, and the villages full of light and life. Israelis went on instilling in their children a feeling of confidence and a love of work and of their fellowmen. Just as the birds came back each morning to twitter around the palm tree split by a shell, just as the cotton bloomed around the shell holes, the lives of her people carried on. What more in her own lifetime could she ask for?

Years before, in accepting the Stephen Wise Award of the American Jewish Congress, she had described her feelings about the course her life had taken, and she had never since had reason to change her mind:

"If one is privileged in one's lifetime to go all the way

from that small room in Pinsk and live in the state of Israel where there is a great workers' movement . . . and the system and way of life of the kibbutz and the moshav; and if a Jewess who was present in that little room lives to be blessed with children and grandchildren living under a system which cannot be surpassed for justice and uprightness, equality and respect for human dignity—what more can a daughter of Israel ask for?

"Perhaps you will think it's pretense—I hope not—but believe me, there has not been a single day of my life when I've said to myself: 'Well, here you are, today you've done something for the people of Israel, for the state of Israel.'

"For myself, after all these things, I desire only one thing more: to live only as long as I can live a full life in the state of Israel, and may I never lose the feeling that it is I who am indebted."

Shalom, Golda!

Bibliography

Agress, Eliyahu. *Golda Meir, Portrait of a Prime Minister*. New York: Sabra Books, 1969.

Borchsenius, Poul. *And It Was Morning*. London: George Allen & Unwin, Ltd., 1962.

Christman, Henry, ed. *This Is Our Strength, Selected Papers of Golda Meir*. New York: The Macmillan Company, 1962.

Comay, Joan. *Ben-Gurion and the Birth of Israel*. New York: Random House, Inc., 1967.

Laquer, Walter, ed. *The Israel-Arab Reader*. New York: Bantam Books, 1969.

Latour, Anny. *The Resurrection of Israel*. Cleveland, Ohio: The World Publishing Company, 1968.

Ribalow, Harold U., ed. *Fighting Heroes of Israel*. New York: The New American Library, Inc., 1967.

Robinson, Donald, ed. *Under Fire: Israel's 20 Year Fight for Survival*. New York: W. W. Norton & Company, Inc., 1968.

Sachar, Morley. *From the Ends of the Earth: The Peoples of Israel*. New York: Dell Publishing Co., Inc., 1970.

Slater, Leonard. *The Pledge*. New York: Simon and Schuster, Inc., 1970.

Syrkin, Marie. *Golda Meir, Israel's Leader*, rev. ed. New York: G. P. Putnam's Sons, 1969.

Teveth, Shabtan. *The Tanks of Tammuz*. London: Sphere Books, Ltd., 1968.

Index

Index

Abdullah, King, 103–108, 110
Africa, relations with, 148–154
Al Fatah, 157, 169, 173–174
Aleichem, Shalom, 30
Allon, Yigal, 161, 164
American Jewish Congress, 40, 192
American Jewish Joint Distribution Committee, 124
American-Jewish youth rally, 185
American Young Sister Society, 10–11
Amman, 106
Anglo-American Commission of Enquiry, 84–86
Aqaba, Gulf of, 140, 142, 159
Arab guerrillas, *see* Fedayeen
Arab League, 103, 105, 114, 143, 169
Arab Legion, 105, 114
Arab Summit Conference (1964), 157
Arafat, Yasir, 169, 173
Attasi, Nureddin al-, 158

Balfour, Lord Arthur, 37

Balfour Declaration, 36–37, 40, 64
Bar-Niv, Zvi, 127–128
Beersheba, 129
Ben-Gurion, David, 35, 39, 65, 67, 75, 88, 99–102, 111, 116, 136, 138–139, 155
Ben-Zvi, Itzhak, 35, 39, 67
Bernadotte, Count Folke, 115, 122
Bernstein, Leonard, 182
Black Sabbath (1946), 88–89
Bloody Sunday (1905), 2
Bunche, Ralph J., 122

Casals, Pablo, 147
Churchill, Sir Winston, 103
Council of Jewish Federations, 98
Cyprus, 87, 91–93, 135
Czechoslovakia, 102, 136

Danin, Ezra, 106–109
Dayan, Moshe, 139–140, 161, 164, 178
Debs, Eugene V., 11
Degania, 48
Denver, 14, 16–17, 20–28
Dinitz, Simcha, 155, 175
D.P. (displaced persons) camps, 84, 91–93
Dostrovsky, Jacob, 101
Dulles, John Foster, 142

Eban, Abba, 117, 171
Egypt (Egyptians), 114–115, 122, 136, 138–141, 160, 166,

174–175, 178, 185, 187–188
Eisenhower, Dwight D., 142
Elath, 140, 159
Eshkol, Levi, 155, 158–161

Feda, 88
Fedayeen, 136, 138, 163, 169–173, 177–178
Federenko, Nikolai, 158
Four Freedoms, 87
France, 148, 159, 167

Gaulle, Charles de, 167
Gaza Strip, 140, 142, 160, 168, 173
Glubb Pasha, 114
Golan Heights, 157, 159–160, 168, 172
Graham, Rev. Billy, 153
Great Britain, 159, 167

Hadassah, 44, 74, 126
    Hospital (Mount Scopus), 101
Haganah, 64, 69, 76, 78–80, 82, 87, 89, 96, 100, 107, 109–110
Haifa, 74, 87, 152
Hebrew University, 74, 147
Hegel, Georg Wilhelm, 21
Herzl, Theodor, 32, 148
Hillel, 33
Hirsch, Baron Moritz, 31
Histadrut, 43, 55, 58, 66–68, 70–72, 78–79, 84
Hitler, Adolf, 69, 75, 77, 80, 98, 141, 191
Hussein, King, 160, 169

Immigrants (immigration)
  Egyptian Jews, 128, 178
  illegal, 75–78, 80, 190
  Iraqi Jews, 128, 129, 173, 177, 192
  Libyan Jews, 173
  to Palestine, 31–32
  resettlement program, 126–129
  Syrian Jews, 178, 192
  vocational training, 134–135
  World War II refugees, 72, 79, 86
  Yemenite Jews, 124–126, 128, 192
Iraq, 114, 129, 173, 177
Irgun Zvai Leumi, 91
Israel
  declaration of independence, 112
  Defense Army, 116, 134, 139–141
    organization of, 139–140
  education in, 176
  first national election, 122
  International Cooperation Program, 150, 152
  Labor party, 63, 68, 110, 155, 161, 165
  recognition by United States, 113
  Sinai Campaign, 139–141
  Six-Day War, 157–161
  Suez Canal cease-fire, 187–189
  War of Independence, 113–116

Jaffa, 44, 68
Jarring, Dr. Gunnar V., 166, 187–188
Jerusalem, 45–46, 59, 94–96, 106, 110, 126, 146, 160, 170, 172, 190
Jerusalem *Post*, 180

Jewish Agency, 45, 65, 86, 88–92, 94, 117
Jewish Brigade, 78
Jewish Hospital for Consumptives, 14
Jewish Legion, 39, 47
Jewish National Fund, 49
Jewish National Home, 64, 69, 74
Johnson, Lyndon B., 159
Jordan, 103, 114, 122, 138, 153, 157, 166, 185
    West Bank, 160, 173

Kadar, Lou, 117, 120
Katzenelson, Berl, 67
Kibbutz, description of, 38, 48
Kiev, 1–4, 7
Kiryat Shemona, 130, 171
Kishinev pogrom, 1, 88
Knesset, 133, 157, 162, 164, 167
Kopelov, Yossel, 40–41, 44–45
Korngold, Sam, 6, 13–14, 16–17, 23, 41, 45
Korngold, Shana Mabovitz, 4–9, 12–14, 16–17, 20, 34, 41,
        55, 60–61, 96–97, 117
Kupat Holim, 68

Labor Zionists, *see* Poalei Zion
Laird, Melvin, 182
Latrun, 88, 114
Lebanon, 143, 157, 171
Levin, Shmarya, 35

Mabovitz, Blume, 4–18, 28, 61

Mabovitz, Golda, *see* Meir, Golda
Mabovitz, Moshe, 3–4, 6–12, 28, 61
MacDonald, Malcolm, 73, 79
Mapai, *see* Israel, Labor party
Marcus, David (Mickey), 116
Mauritius, 76
Mea Shearim, 60
Medzini, Regina Hamburger, 10, 12, 14–17, 26, 34, 39–40, 44–45, 60–61, 114–115, 117, 162
Meir, Gideon, 184
Meir, Golda
  Abdullah, King, and, 103–108
  African tours, 148–154
  ambassador to Moscow, 116–121
  Anglo-American Commission of Enquiry and, 84–86
  automobile accident, 116
  childhood in Kiev and Pinsk, 1–7
  children, birth of, 59, 61
  Cyprus internment-camp crisis, intervention in, 91–93
  dates Moshe Meyerson, 25–28
  Denver
    runs away to, 16–17
    school and work in, 20–28
  Foreign Minister of Israel, 137–155
  Hebraizes name, 141
  Histadrut, employment at, 66, 68, 78
  hunger strike, participation in, 88
  in Jerusalem, 59–63
  Jewish Agency, head of political department of, 89–91
  Labor Zionists, joins, 31–37
  Mapai, Secretary-General of, 157
  marriage, 39
  Merhavia

first stay, 47–57
return to, 59–60
Milwaukee Normal School for Teachers, entrance into, 28
Minister of Labor of Israel, 122–135
Moetzot Hapoalot secretary, 63
Nixon, Richard, visit with, 179–184
Palestine, departure for, 41–43
Poalei Zion, organizer for, 39–40
Prime Minister, 165–193
  interim, 162–164
proclamation of independence, signer of, 112
retirement
  first, 155, 157
  second, 161
Sirkin-Richlin trial, testimony in, 79–80
in Tel Aviv, 44–46
United Nations, first address before, 141
United States
  arrival in, 7
  fund-raising tours in, 97–100, 113, 132
  speech tour for Pioneer Women in, 65
Merhavia, 47–57, 59–60, 90
Meyerson, Ayah, 147, 161
Meyerson, Golda, *see* Meir, Golda
Meyerson, Menahem, 59, 65, 81–82, 90, 147, 157, 161
Meyerson, Moshe, 25–28, 33, 35–36, 38–41, 44–47, 56–57, 59–62, 81, 117
Meyerson, Sara, 61, 65, 81–82, 90–91, 101, 117, 122, 139, 147
Milwaukee, 7–19, 85, 173, 185–186
Milwaukee Normal School for Teachers, 28
Moetzot Hapoalot, 63, 77
Mufti of Jerusalem (Amin el-Husseini), 64, 69, 99, 103, 105
Mussolini, Benito, 77

Nahal units, 140
Naharayia, 103, 106, 109
Nasser, Gamal Abdel, 136, 139, 142, 157, 159, 168–169, 174–175, 178, 187
National Insurance Law, 133, 154
National Press Club, 182
Nazareth, 51, 133
Nixon, Richard M., 176, 178–184

Ocean Vigour, 92
Operation Magic Carpet, 124

Palestine
    Arab riots in, 41–42, 63–64, 69–70, 94–96
    Arab strength (1948), 97
    British Mandate, 40, 43–45, 63–64, 69, 71, 73, 76, 78, 81, 83, 86, 89–91, 94, 106
    immigration to, 31–32
    as part of Ottoman Empire, 32, 43
    partition of, 93
    refugees, 142–145, 174
Palestine Liberation Organization, 157, 169–170
Palestine Symphony Orchestra, 90
Patria, 76
Pincus, David, 112
Pinsk, 2–7, 9
Pioneer Women, 63, 65
Poalei Zion, 33, 35, 39–41, 133
Pocahontas, 41–43, 190
Project Nachson, 68–69

Rabin, Itzhak, 160–161, 182
Rabinovitsch, Ben, 147–148
Rahamim, Mordechai, 163
Refugees, *see* Immigrants (immigration)
Revivim, 90, 101, 117, 139, 147, 157, 163, 182
Rothschild, Baron Edmond de, 31
Ruhama, 89

Sadat, Anwar el-, 187
Samuel, Sir Herbert, 64
Saudi Arabia, 169
Schopenhauer, Arthur, 22
Shapiro, Eiga, 117–119
Sharett, Moshe, 89, 96, 117, 136
Sharm-el-Sheikh, 159
Sinai Campaign, 140–141, 158–159
Sinai Peninsula, 139–140, 159, 168
Sirkin-Richlin trial, 79
Six-Day War, 157–161, 166, 168–169, 174, 177, 185
Soviet Jewry, 119–121
Soviet Union, 116, 118, 121, 158, 167, 174, 187
Stern, Clara Mabovitz, 4, 9, 10, 98
Stern, Isaac, 182
Stern gang, 91
Suez Canal, 138, 174–175, 187
Syria, 114–115, 122, 138, 157–160, 166, 172, 177–178, 185
Syrkin, Nachman, 35, 39–40
Szold, Henrietta, 44

Tel Aviv, 44, 46, 58, 60, 96, 106, 111, 141, 172

Thant, U, 159
Trans-jordan, *see* Jordan
Truman, Harry S, 84, 86, 113

United Jewish Appeal, 113
United Nations Emergency Force, 159
United Nations Partition Resolution, 93–94
United Nations Security Council, 115, 141, 166, 169
United Nations Truce Supervision Organization, 158
United States, 97, 113, 132, 160, 167, 176–184, 187–188

Versailles Peace Conference, 40

War Economic Advisory Council, 78
War of Independence (1948–1949), 113–116
Weizmann, Dr. Chaim, 4, 36, 74–75, 117
Weizmann Institute of Science, 74
White Paper of 1939, 73–75, 79, 81–82, 86, 123, 134
Women's Labor Act, 133
Women's Labor Council, *see* Moetzot Hapoalot
Workers' Sick Fund, *see* Kupat Holim
World War I, 29–30, 49
World War II, 69, 76, 82, 100, 134
World Zionist Organization, 32, 68, 74

Yadin, Yigael, 101
Yassky, Dr. Haim, 101
Yemen, 124, 126

Zangwill, Israel, 190